ADULT COLORING BOOK

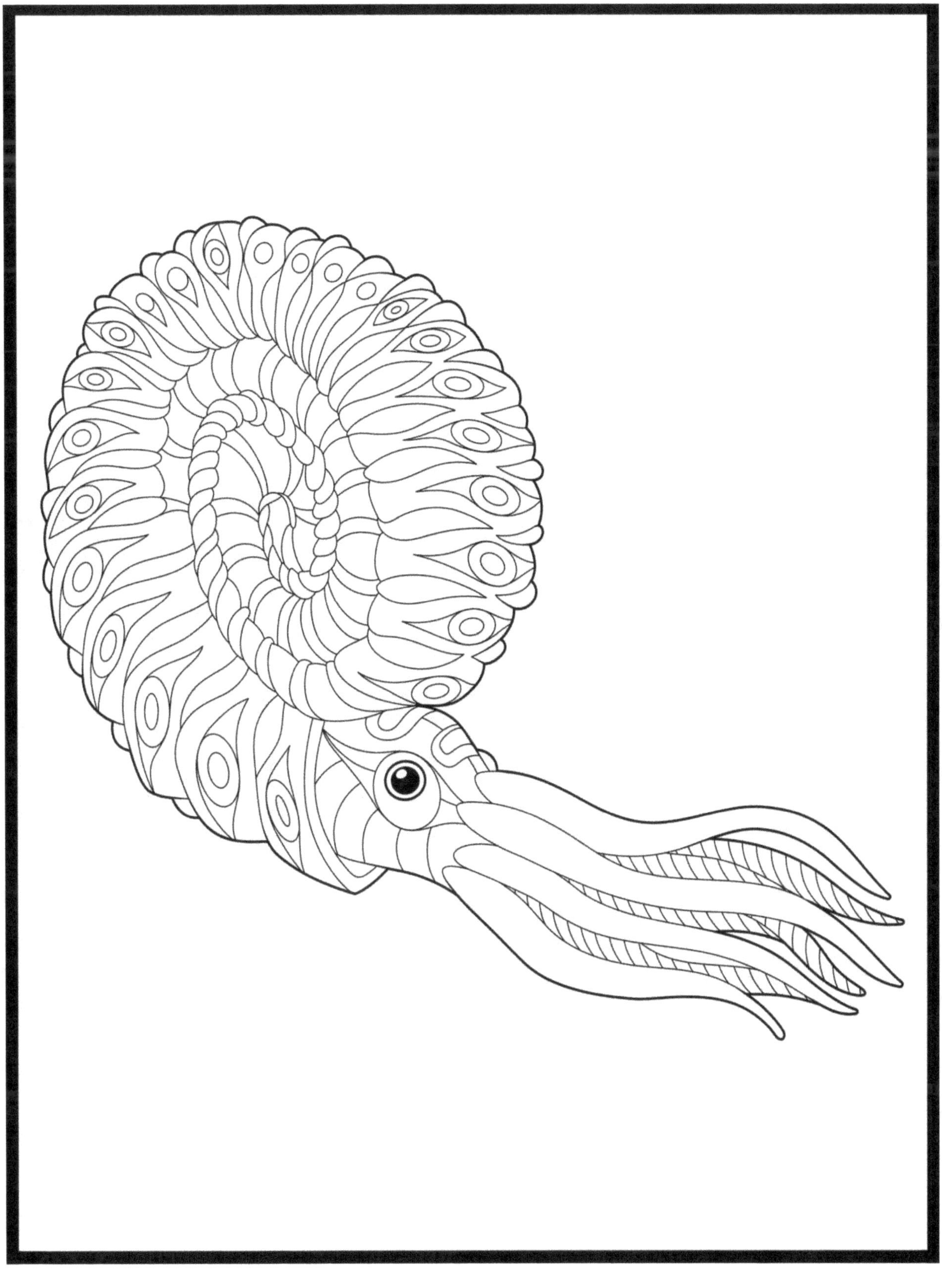

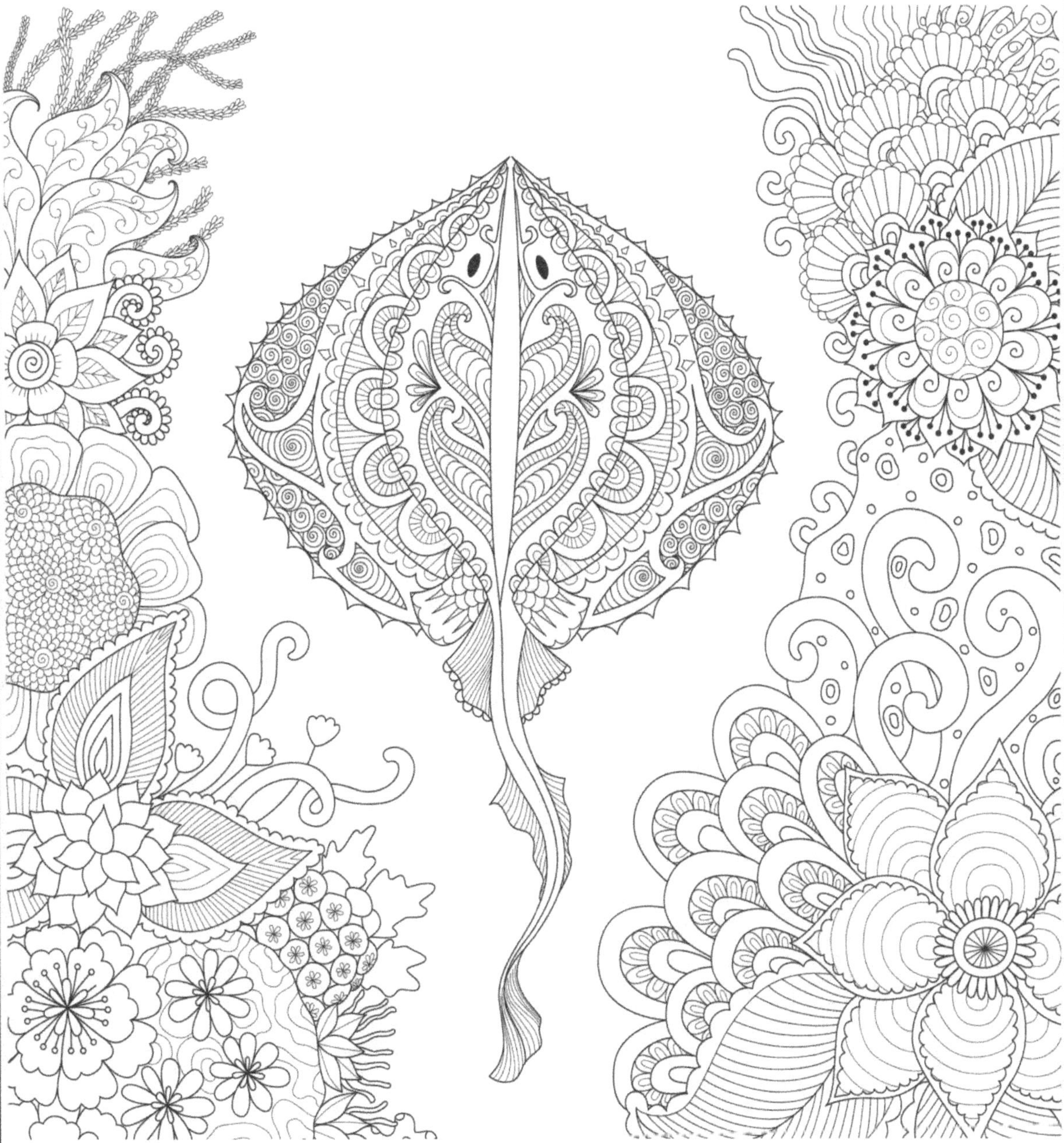

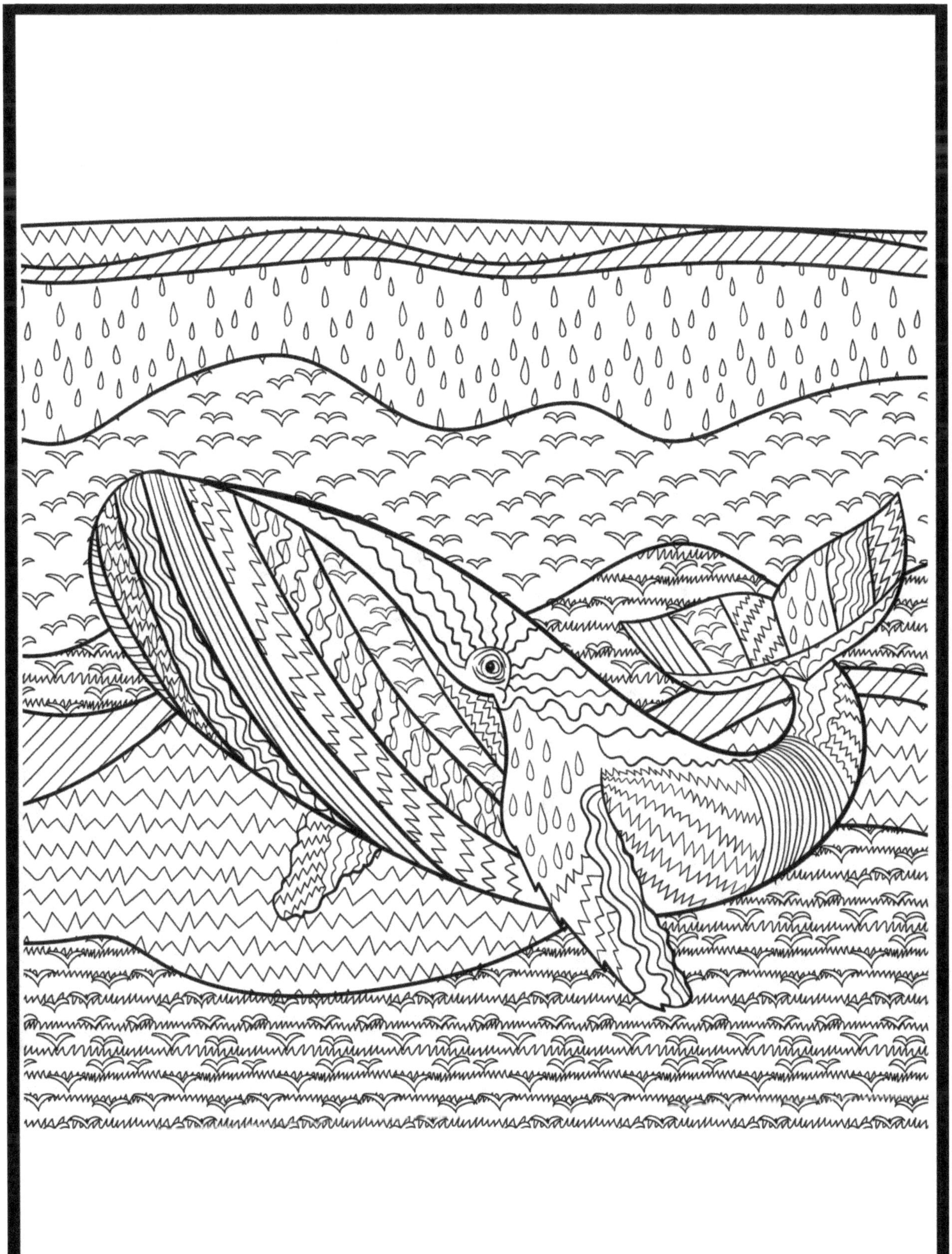

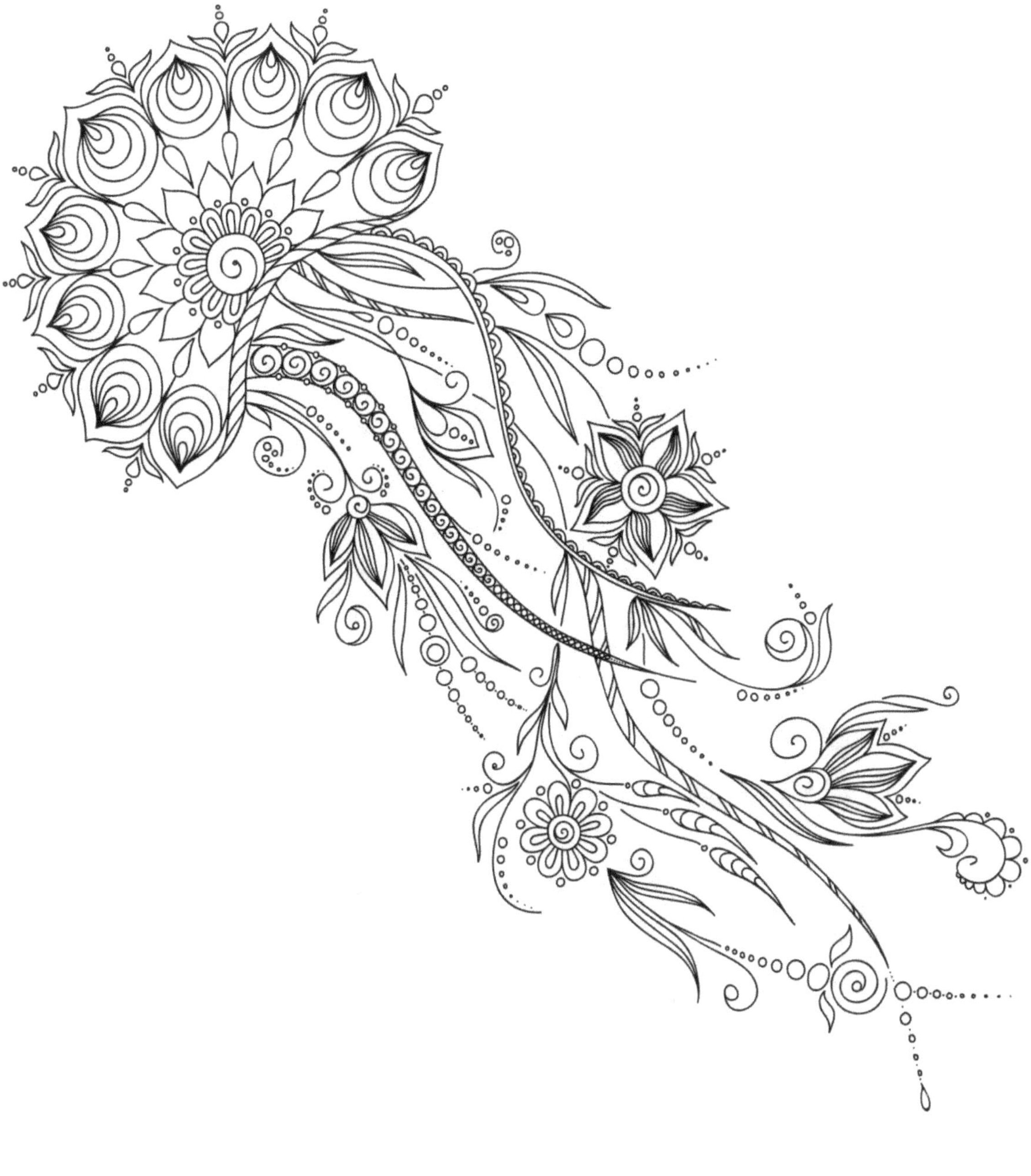

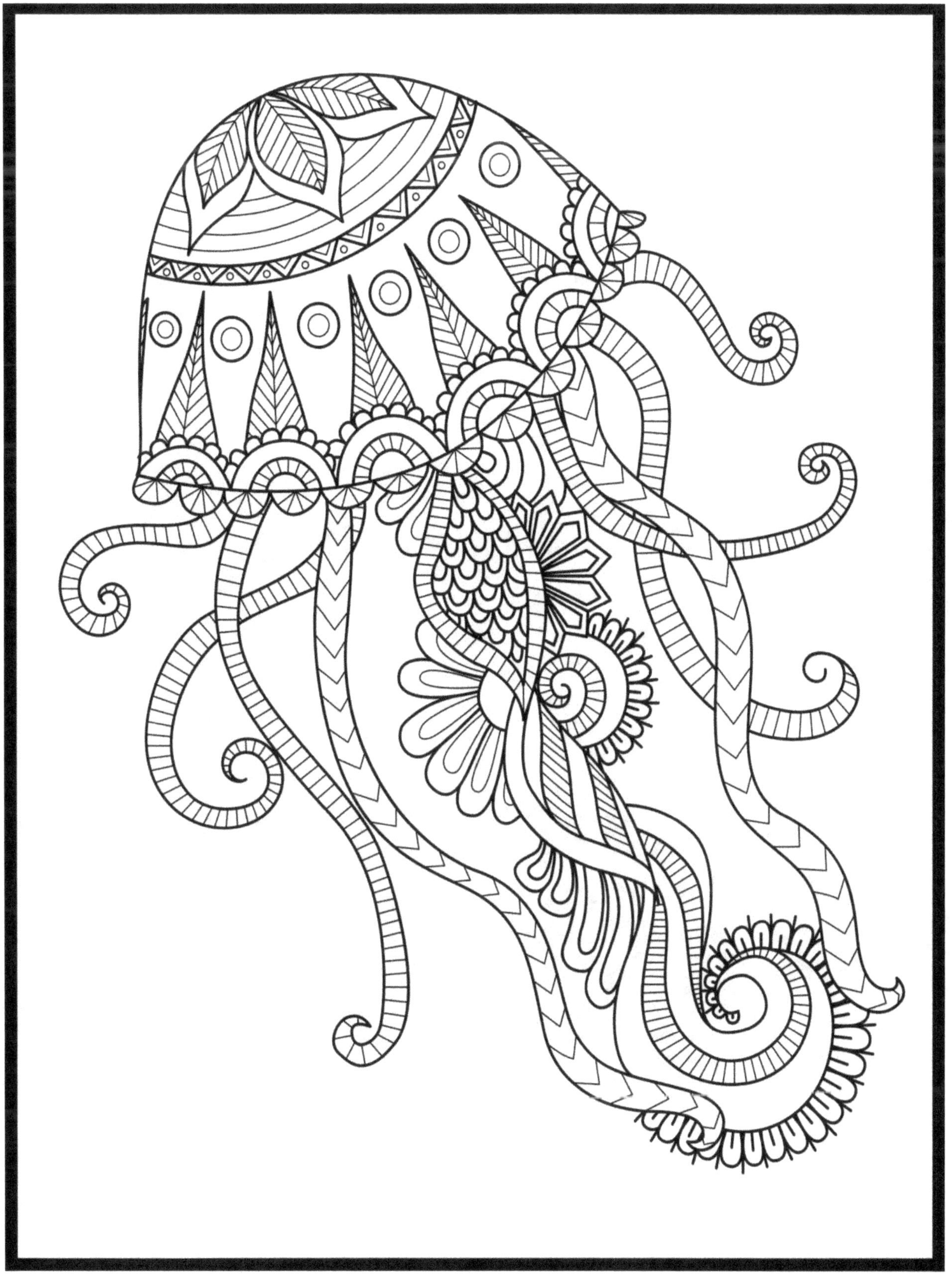

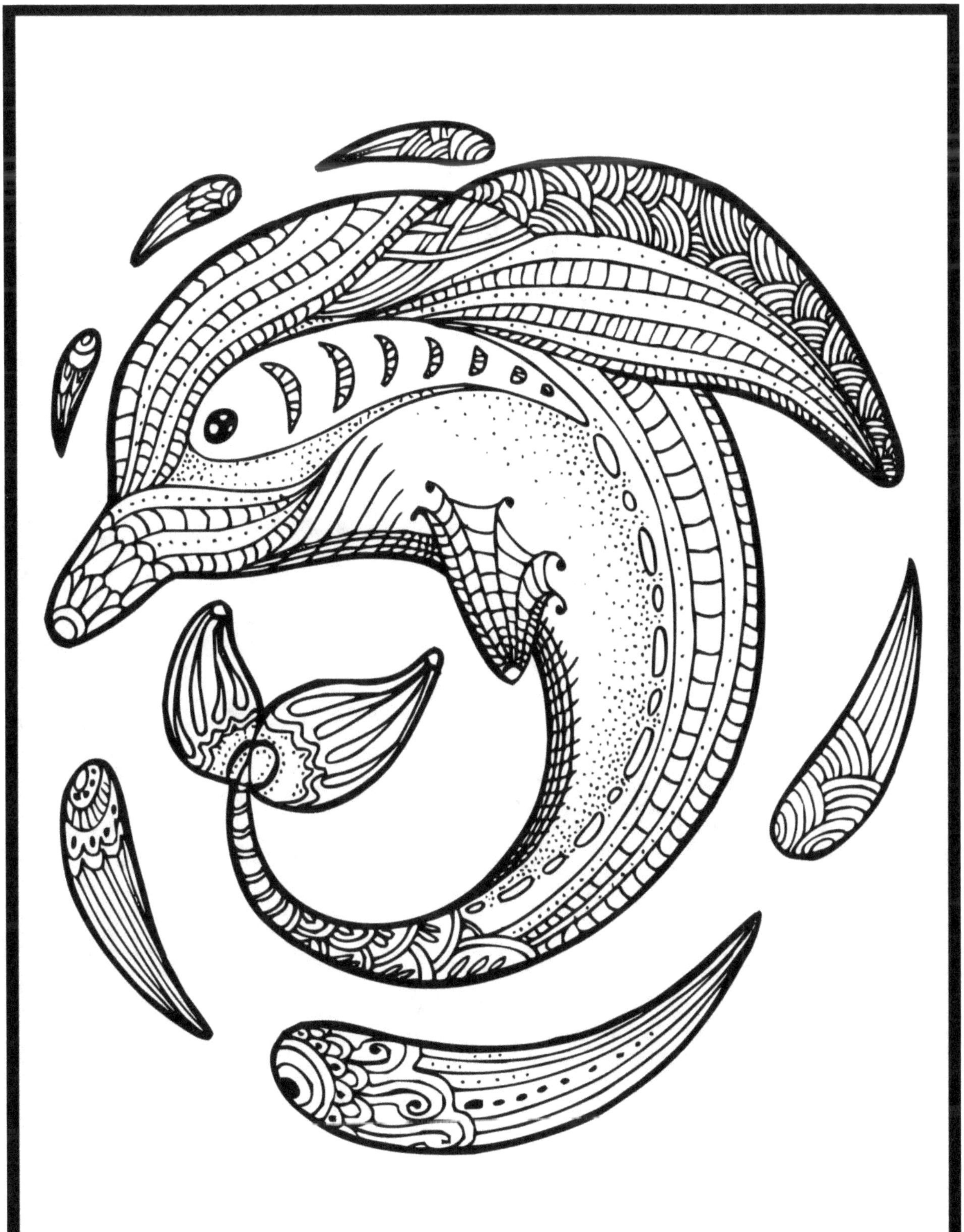

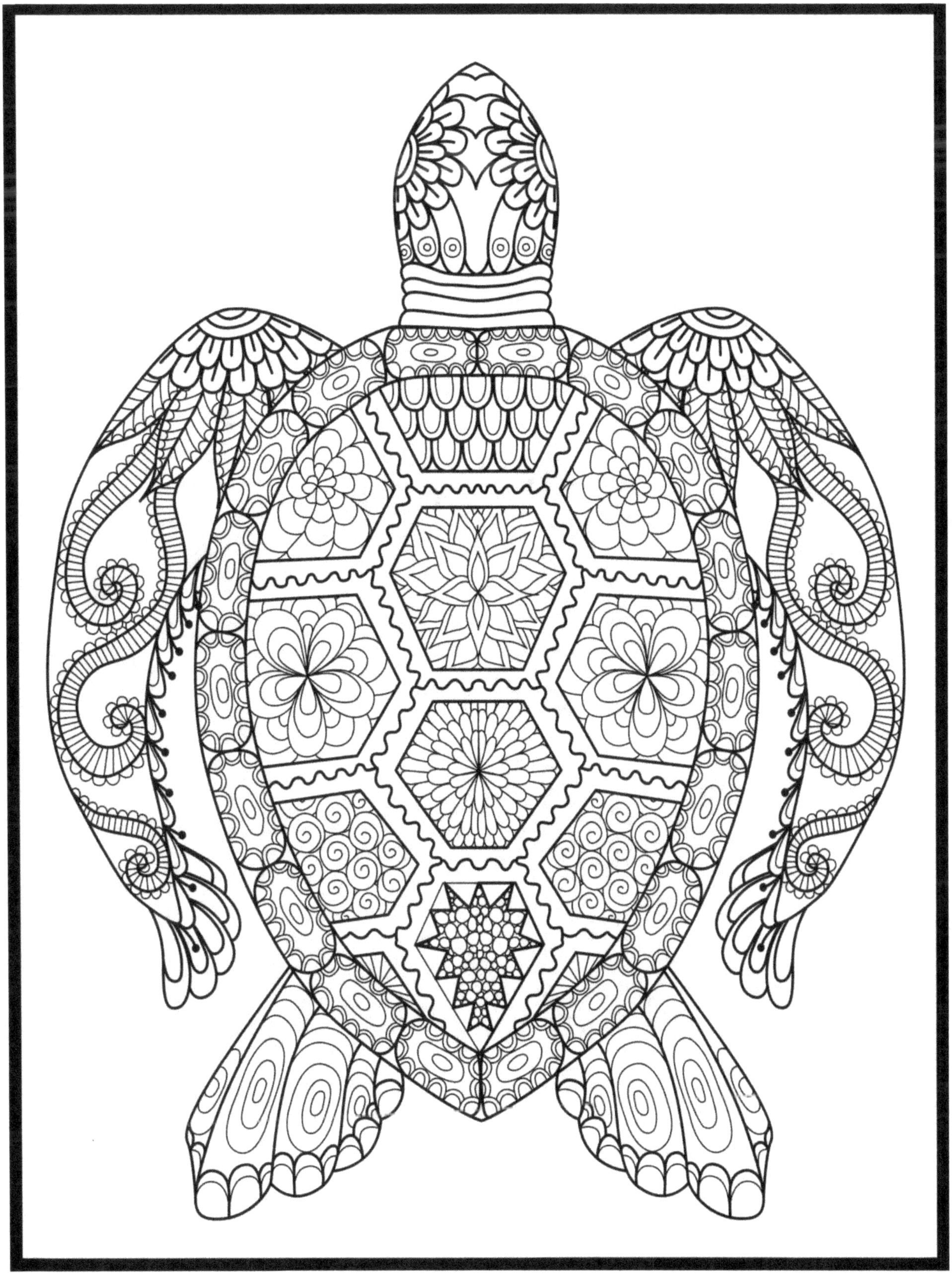

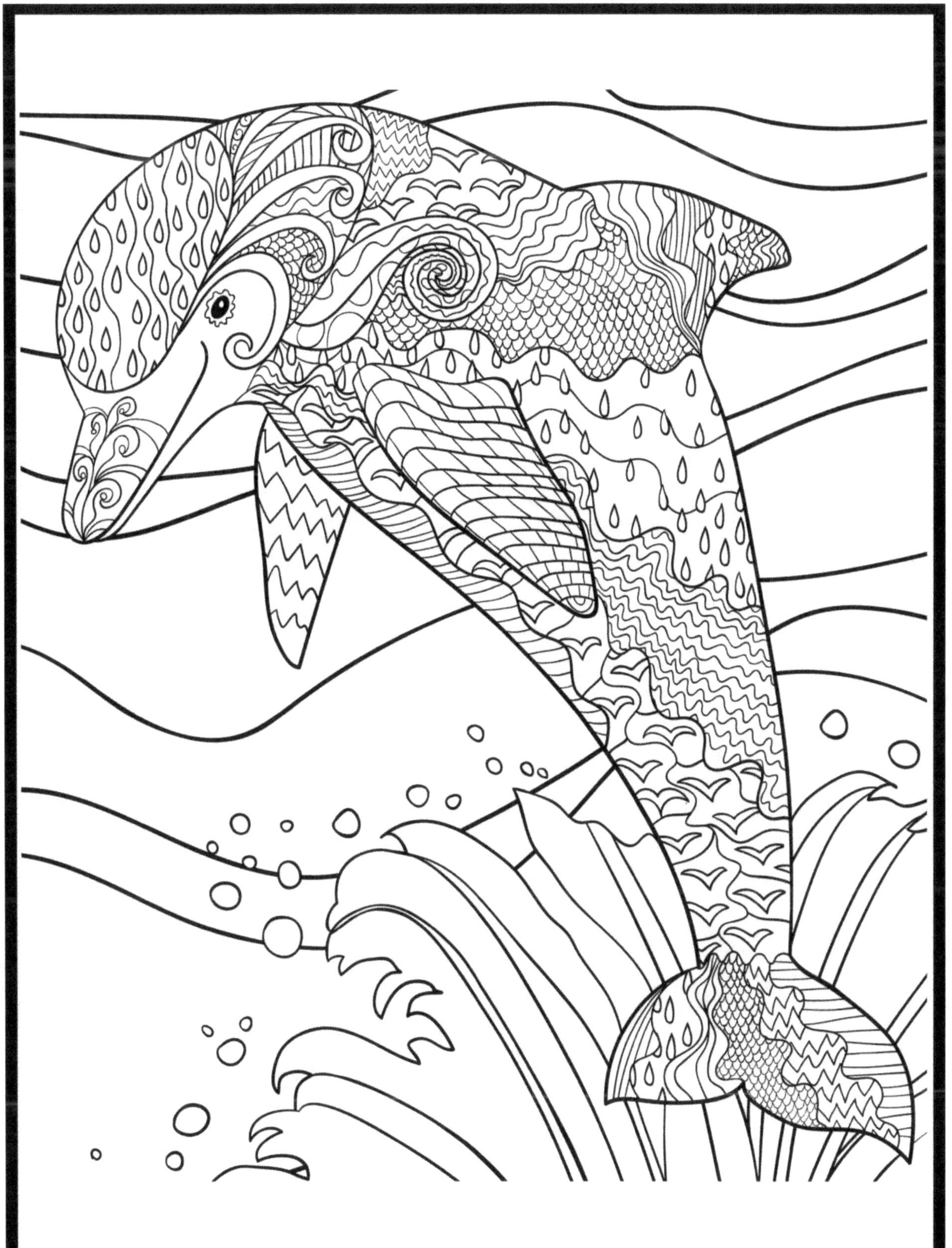

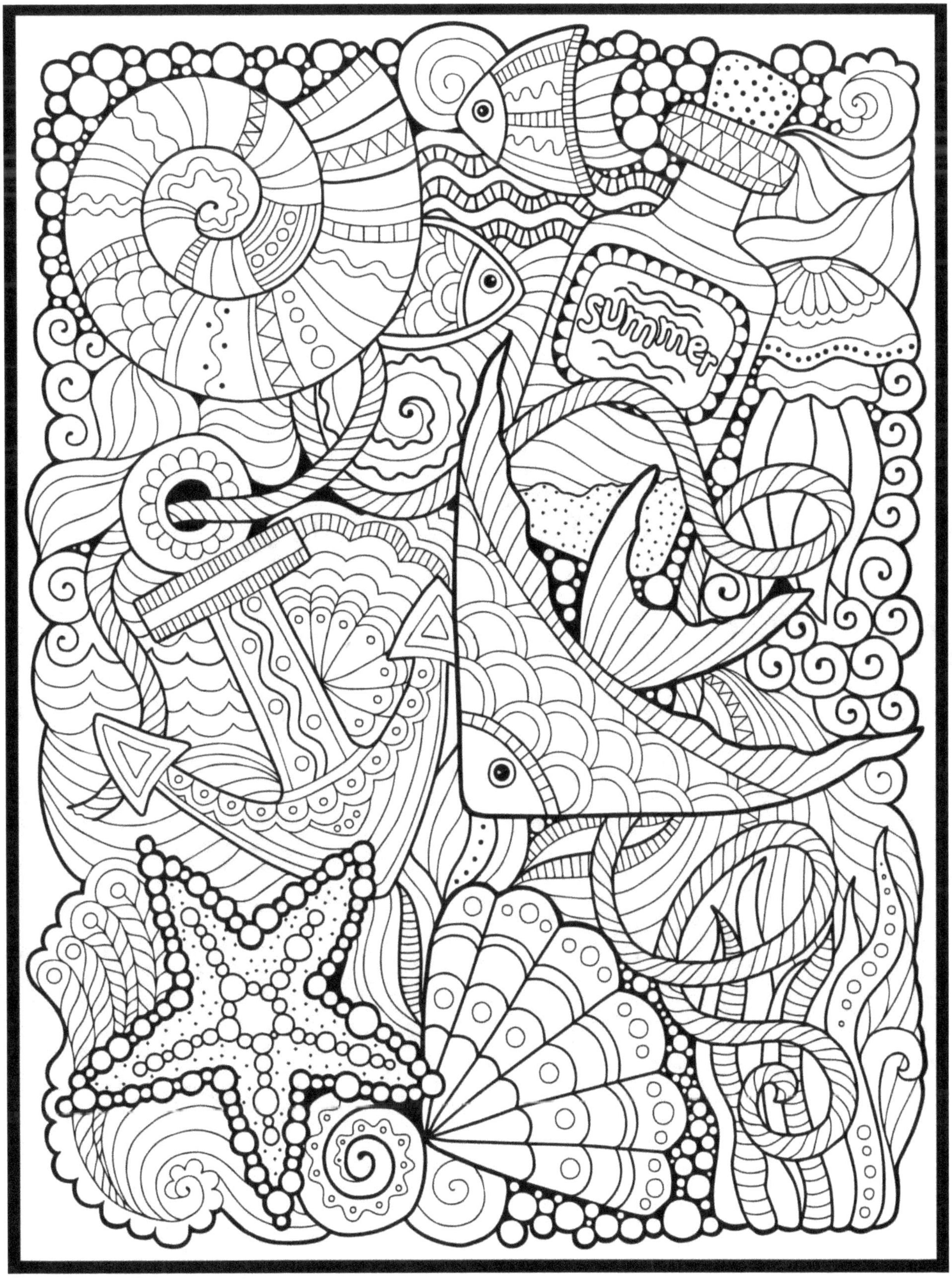
summer

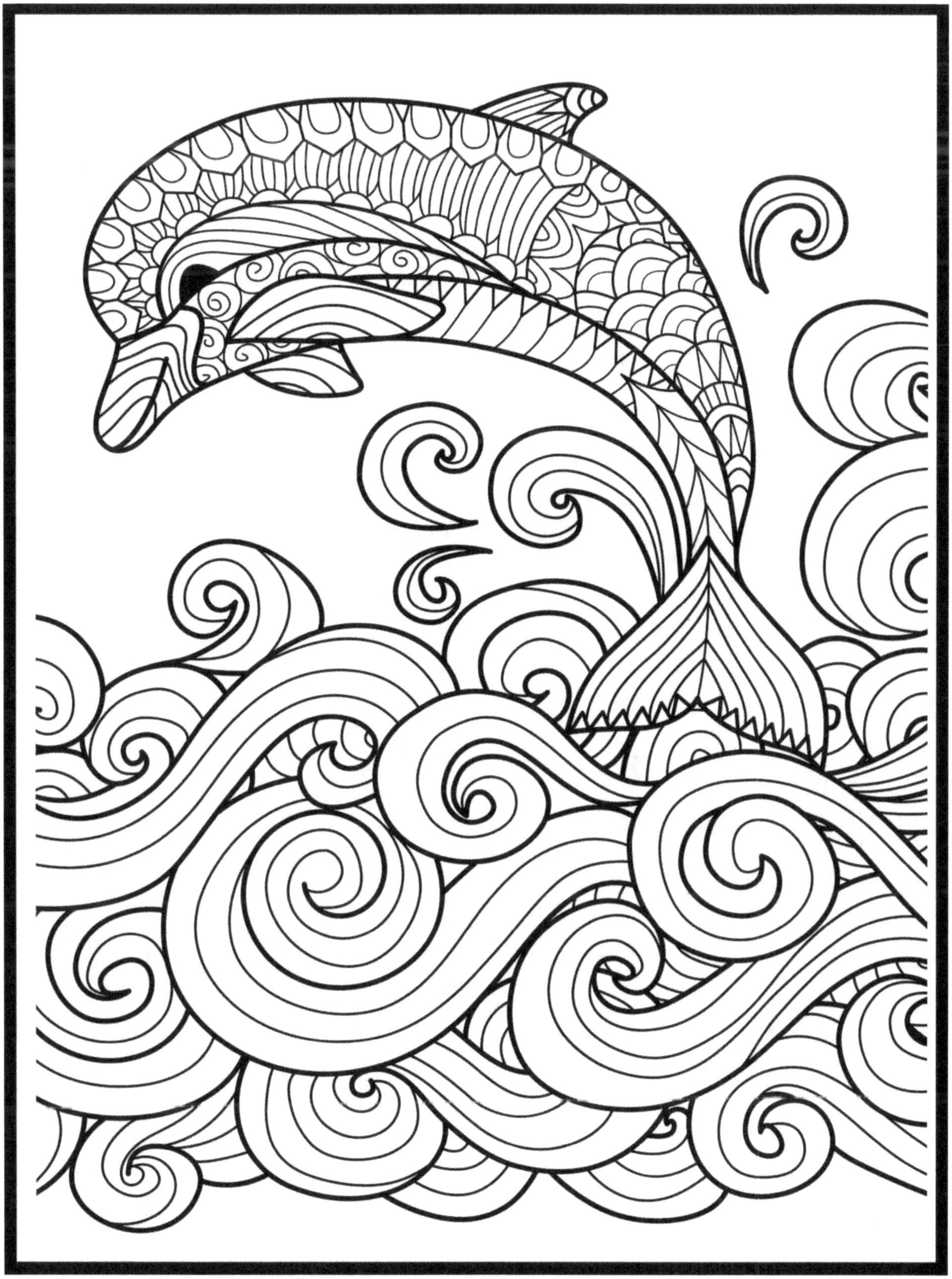

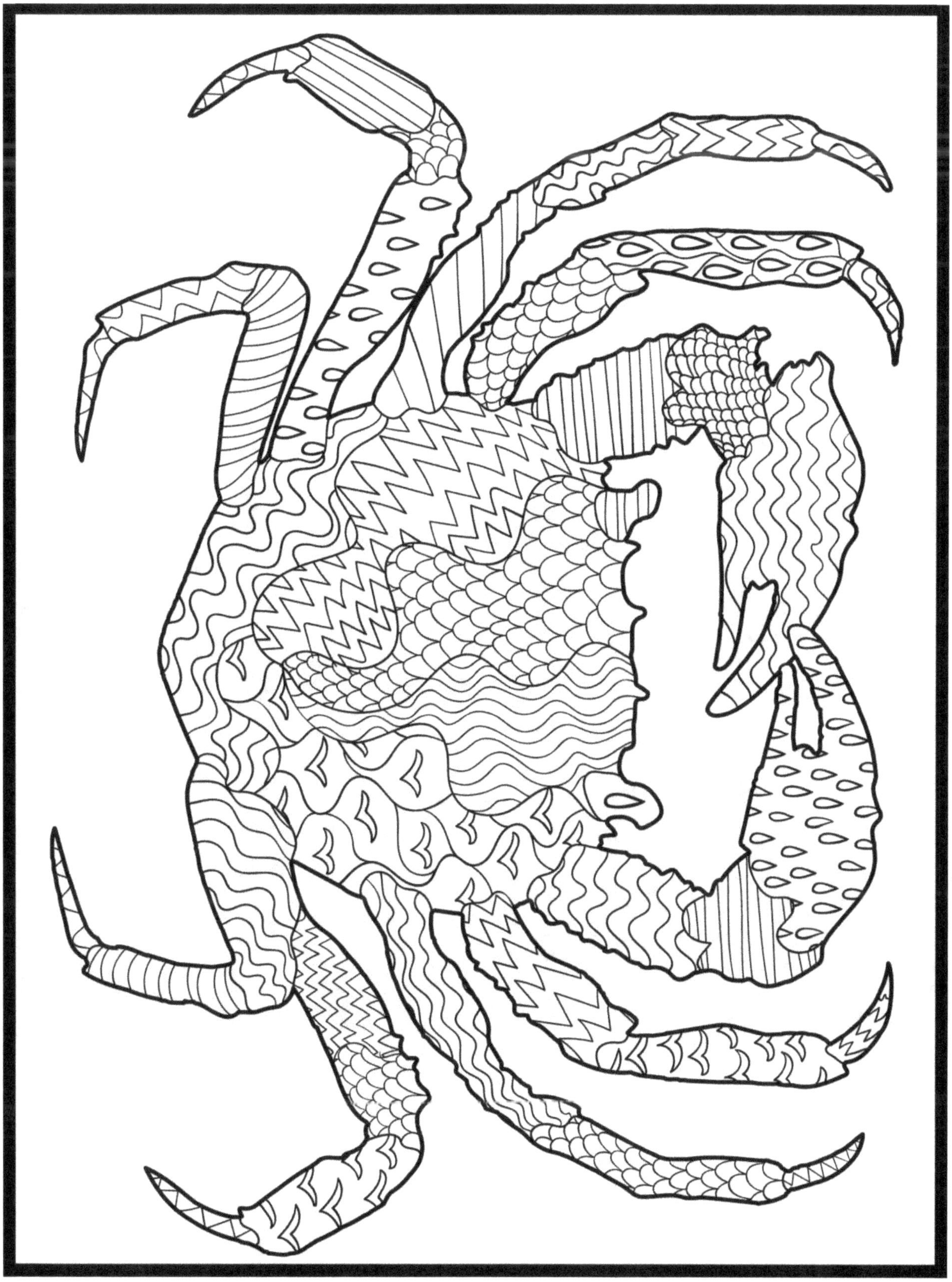

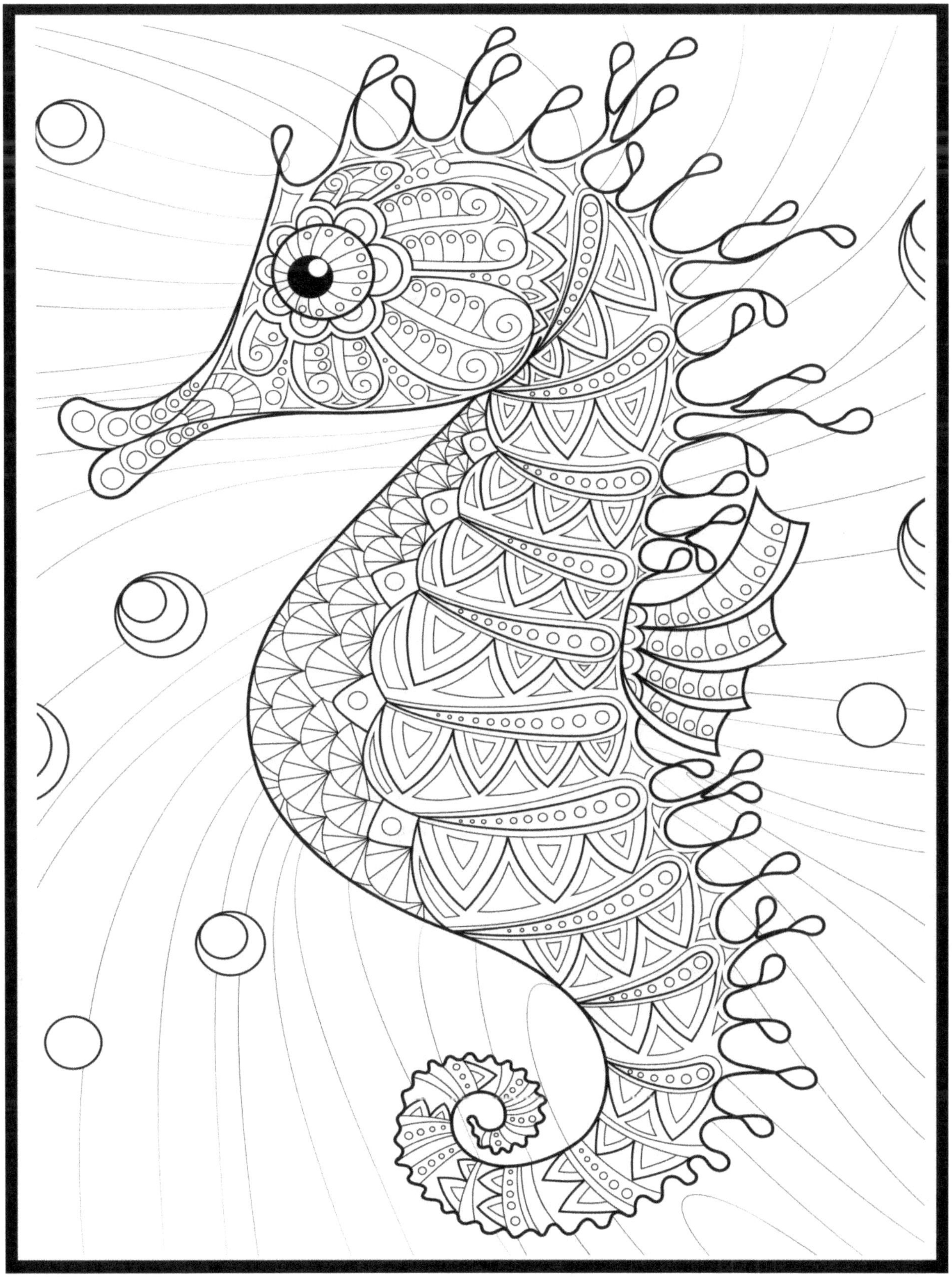

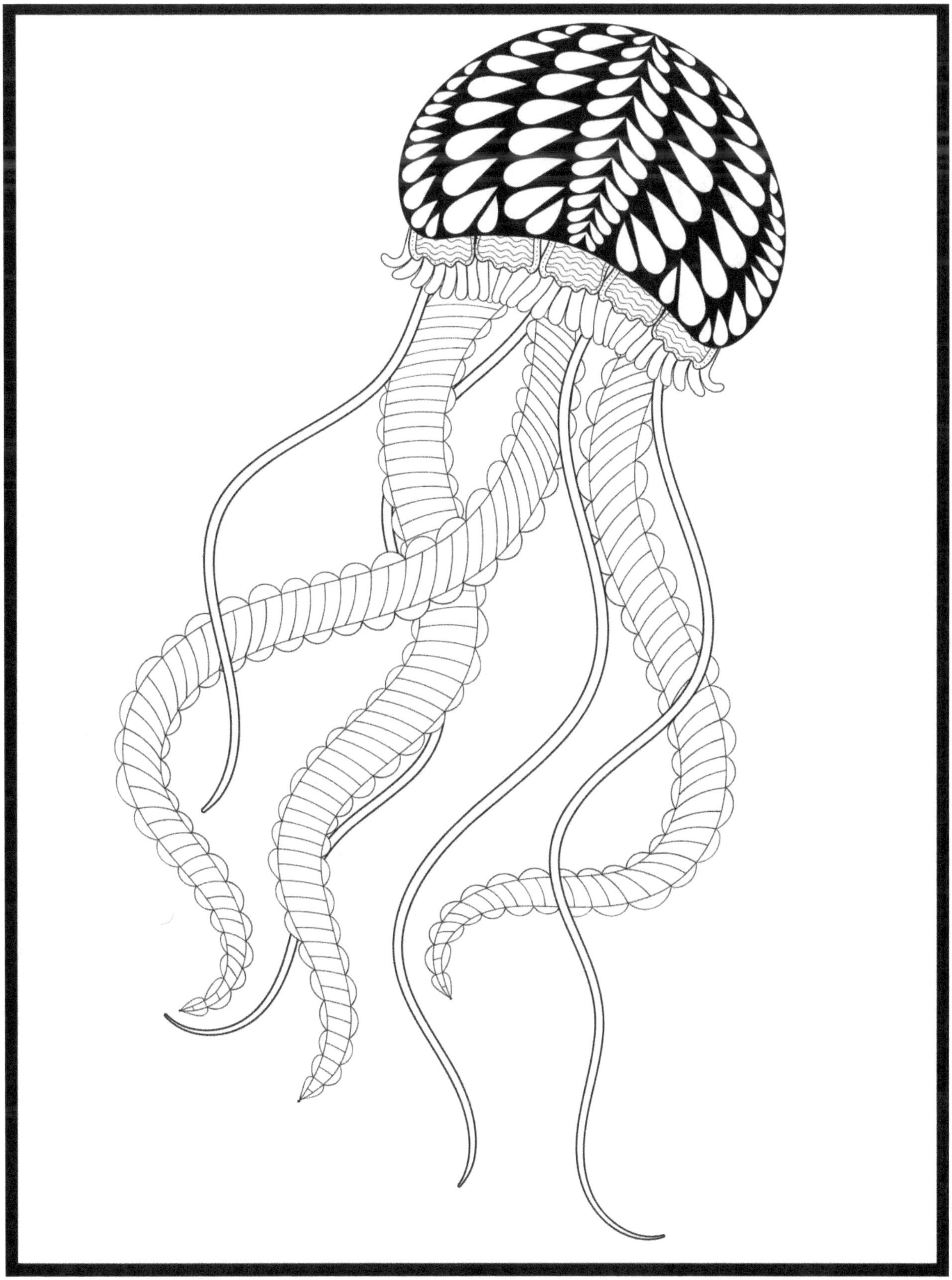

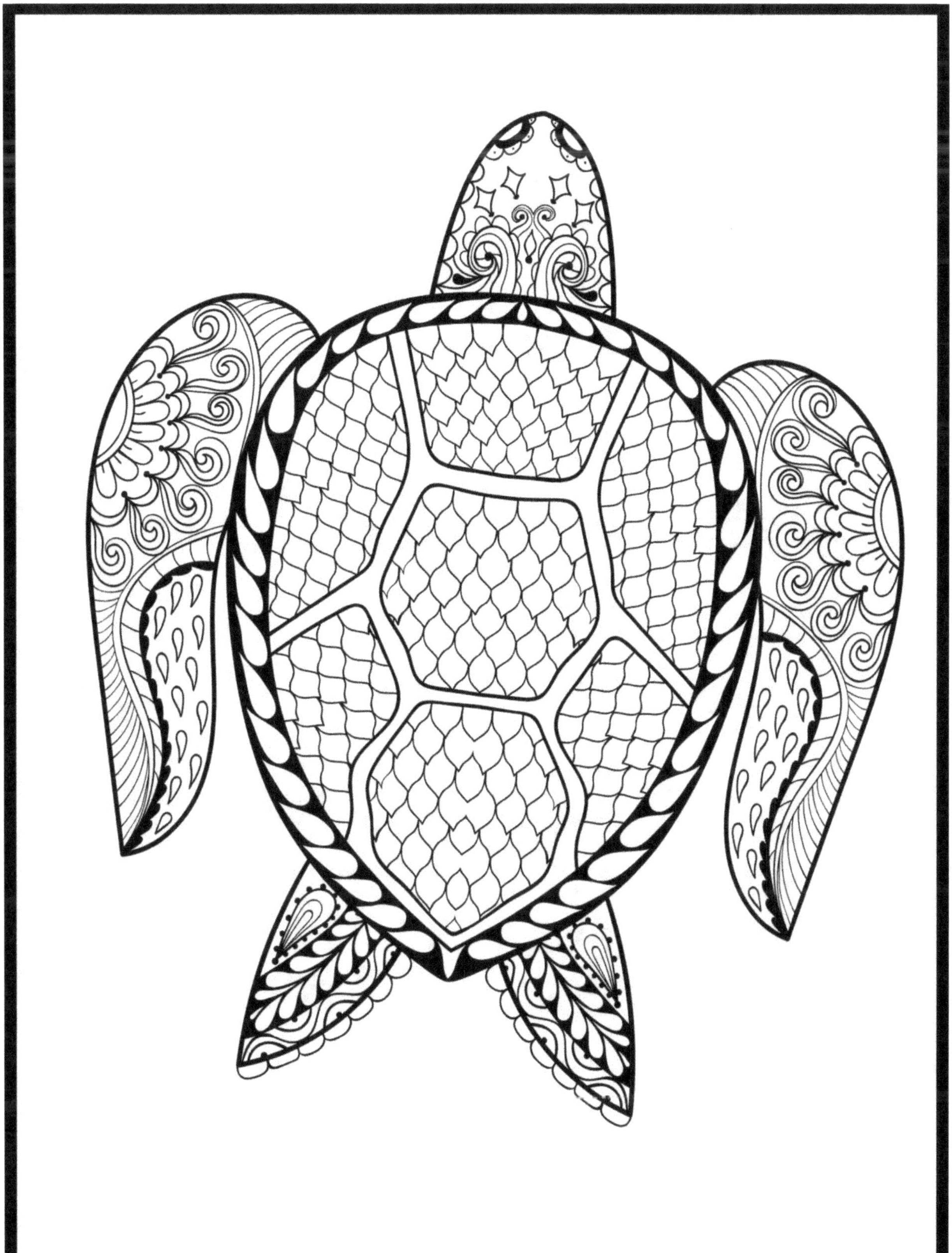

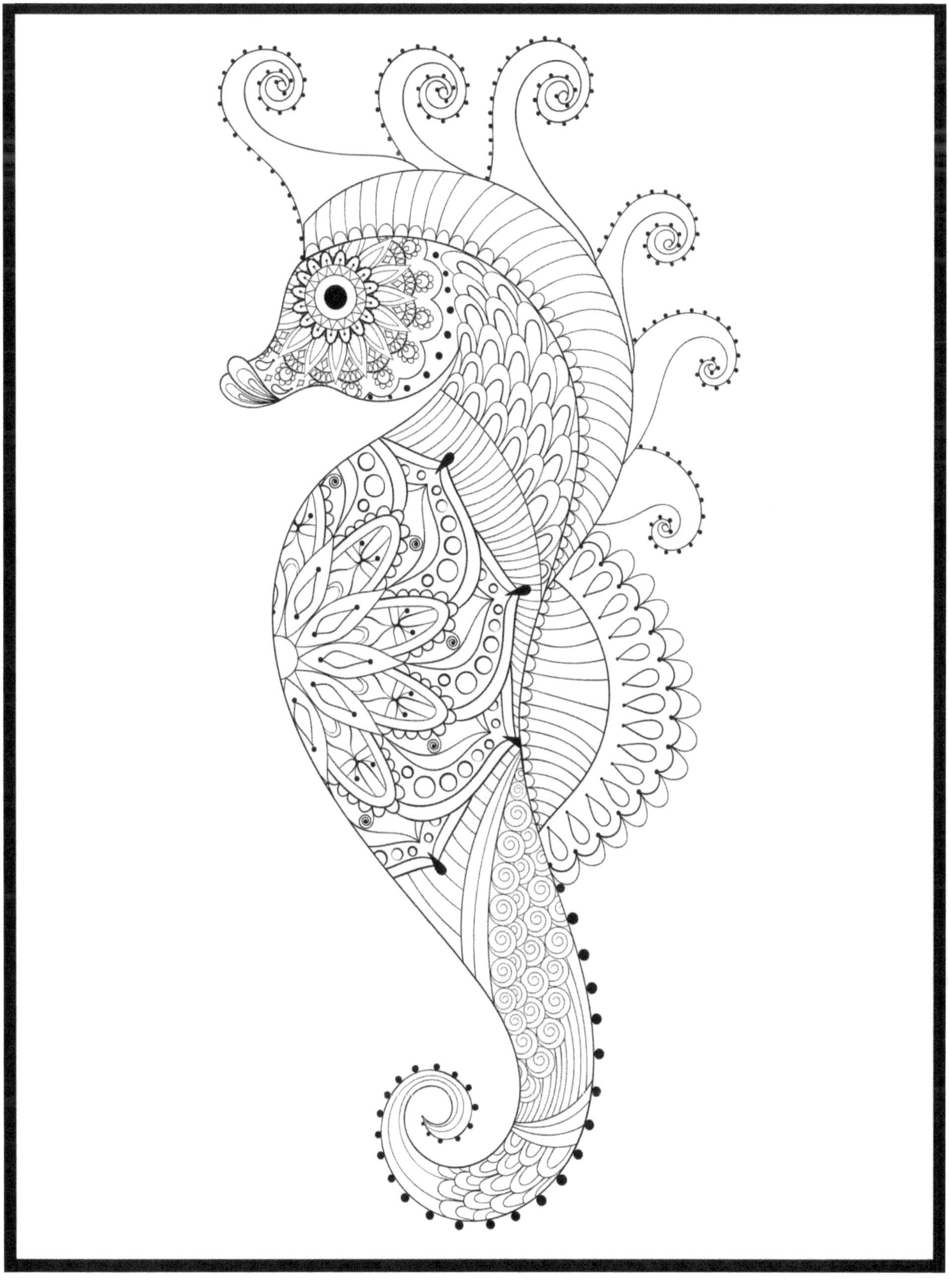

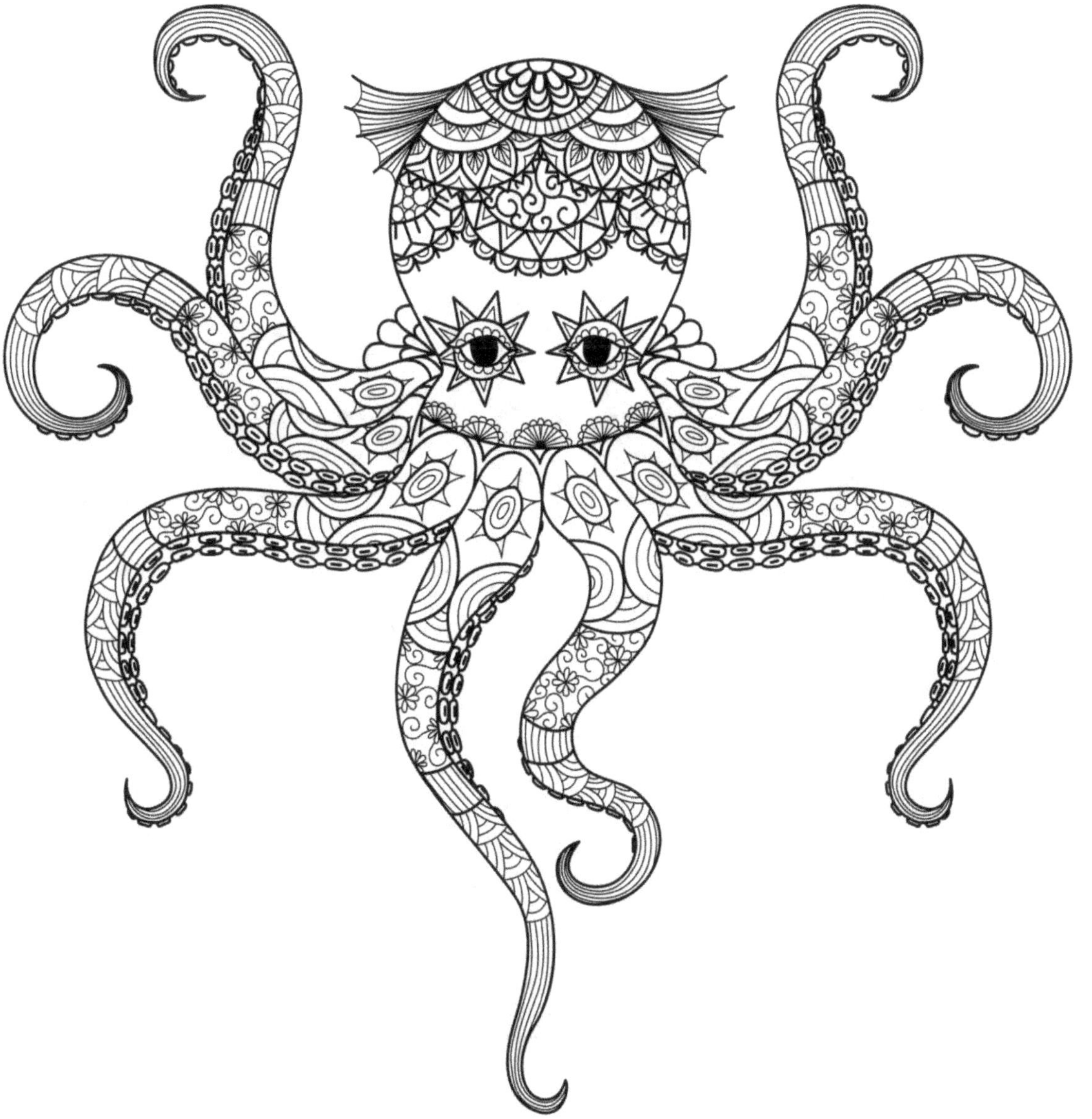

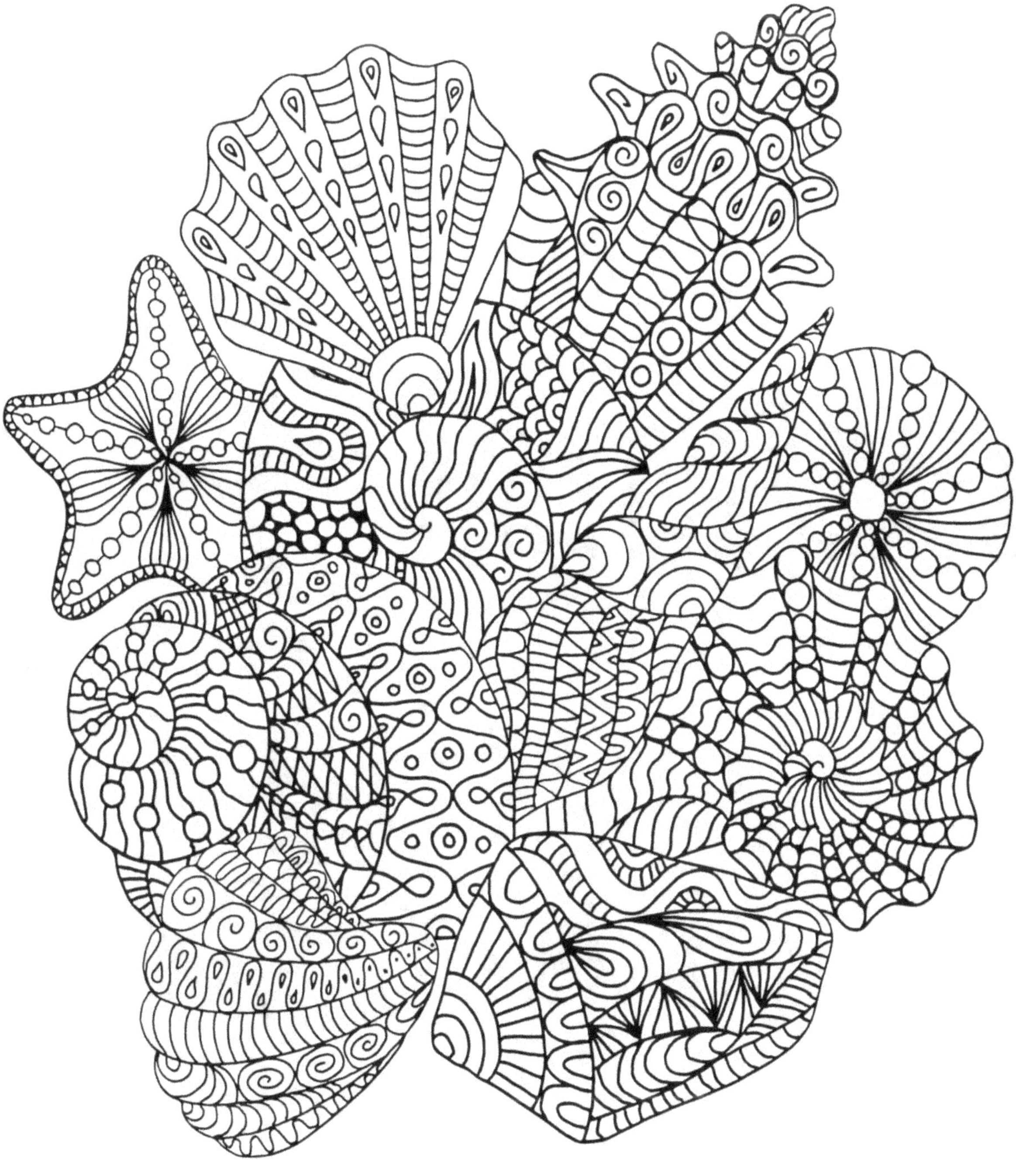

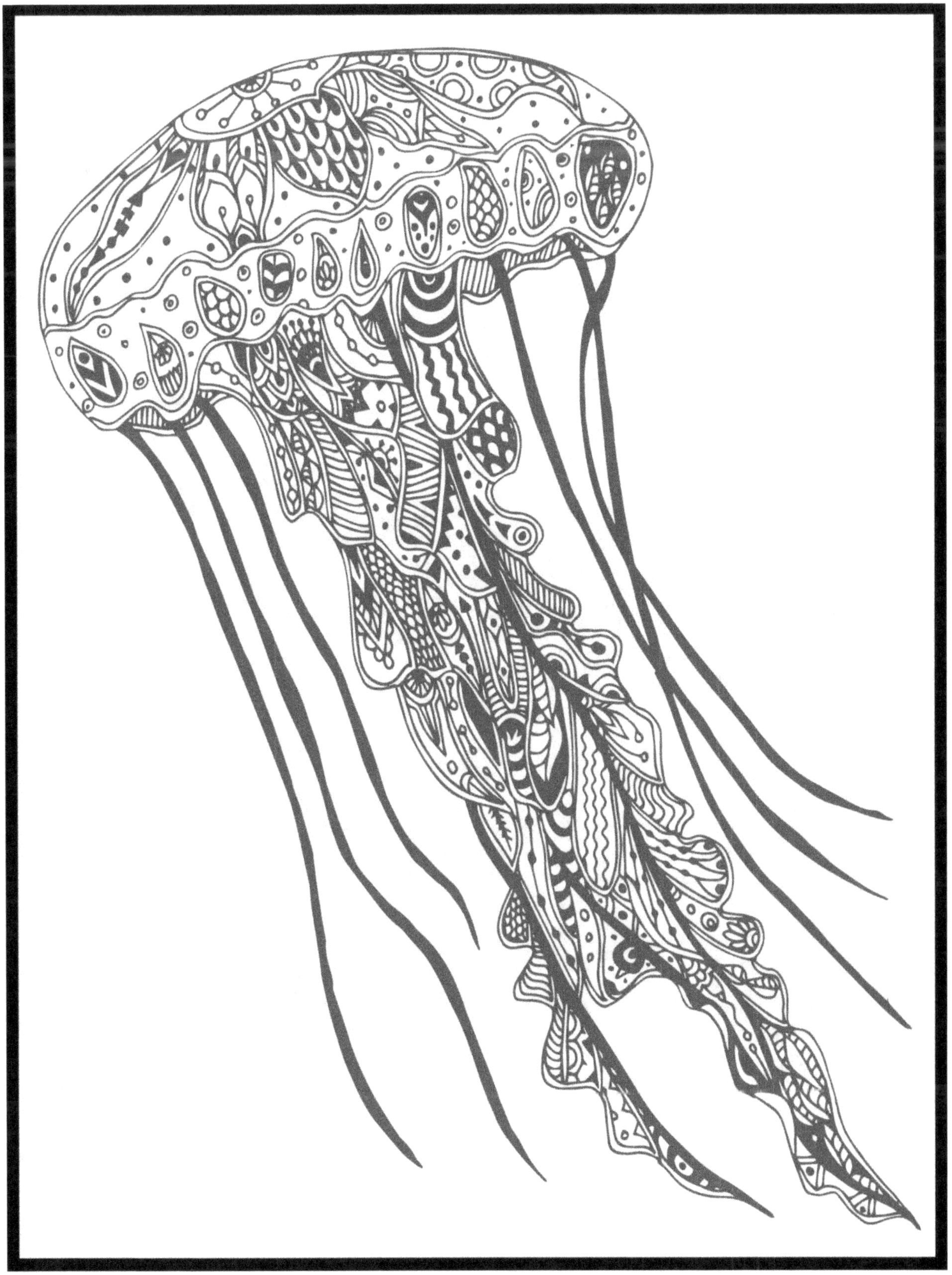

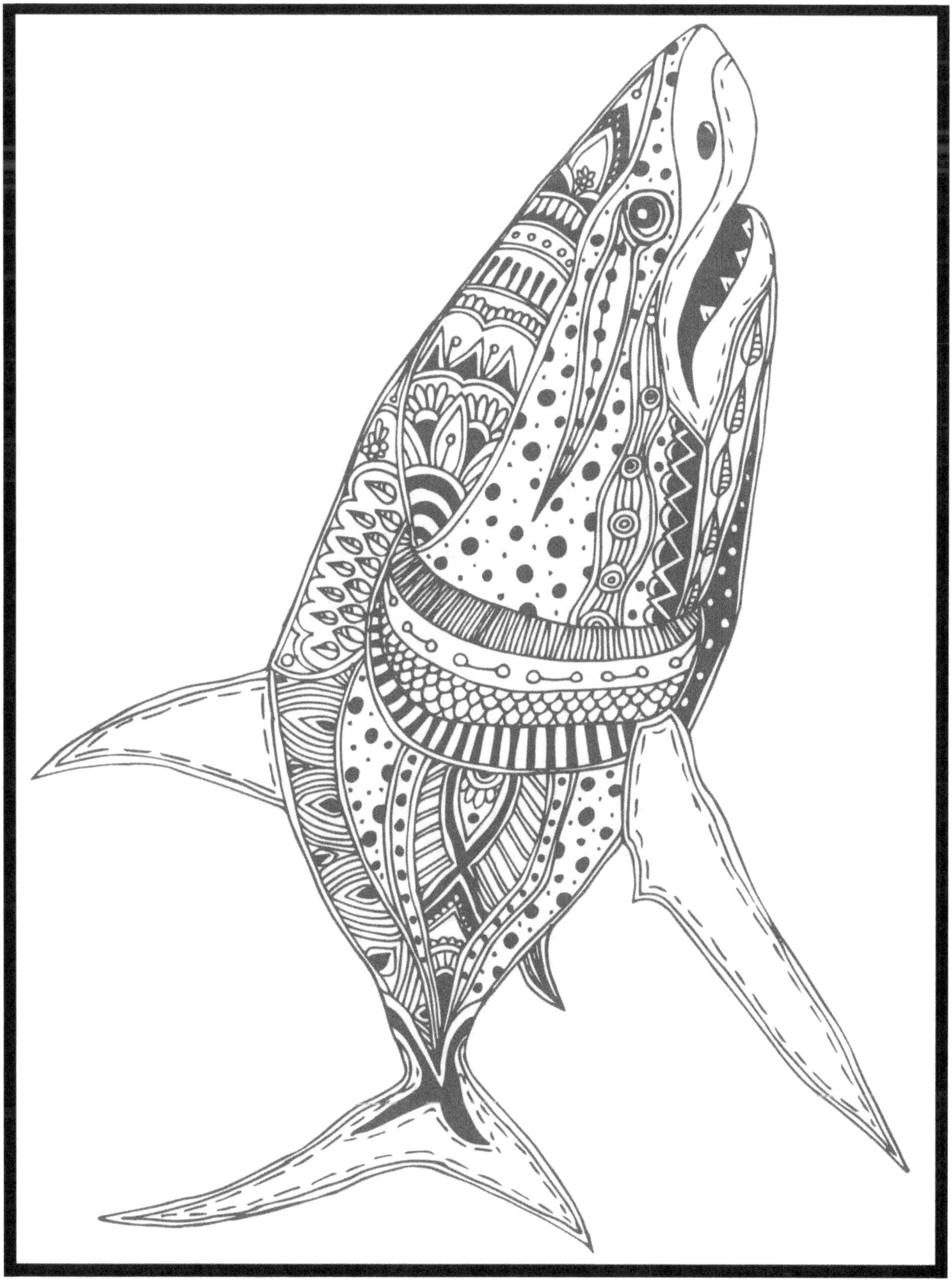

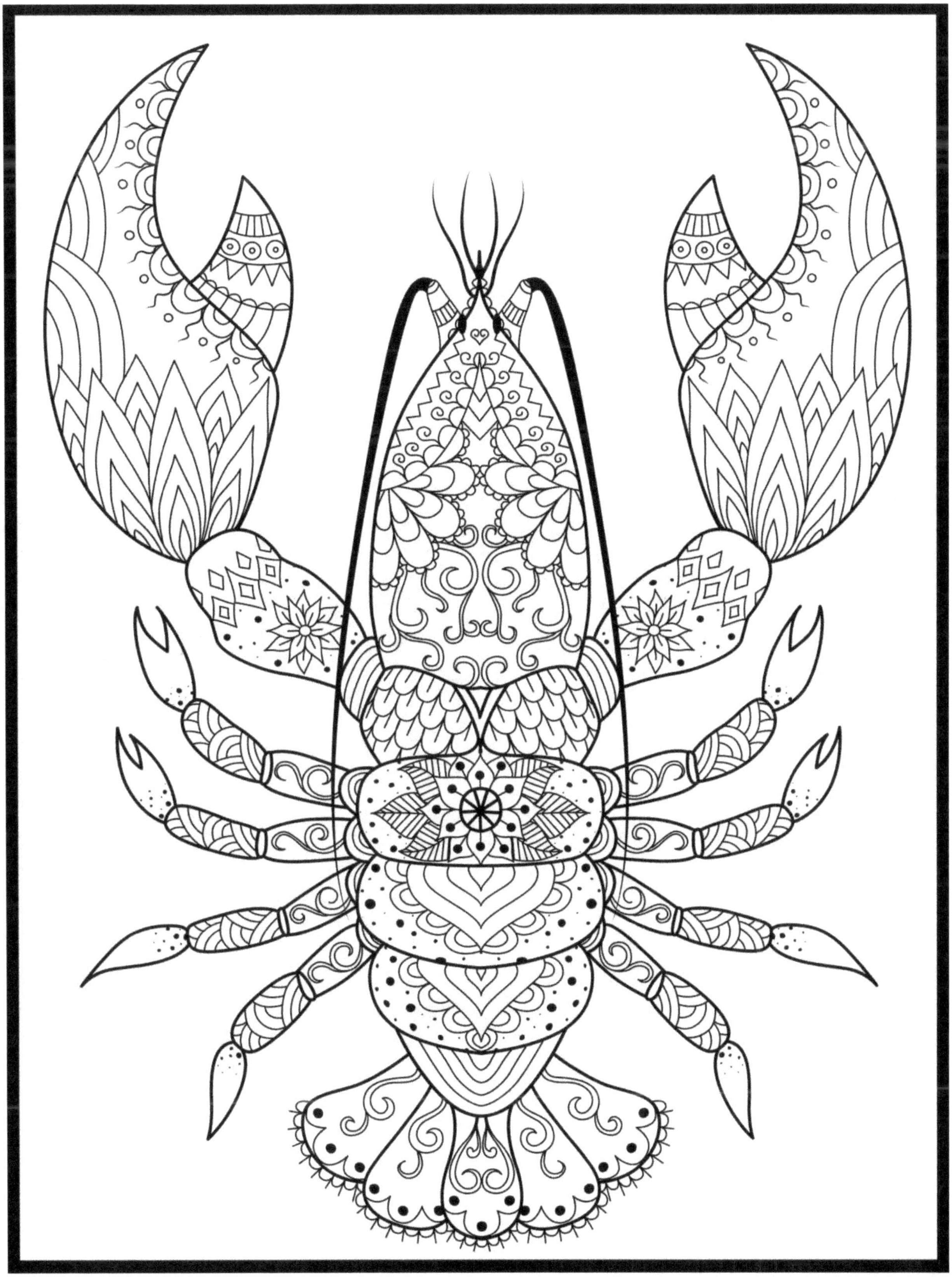

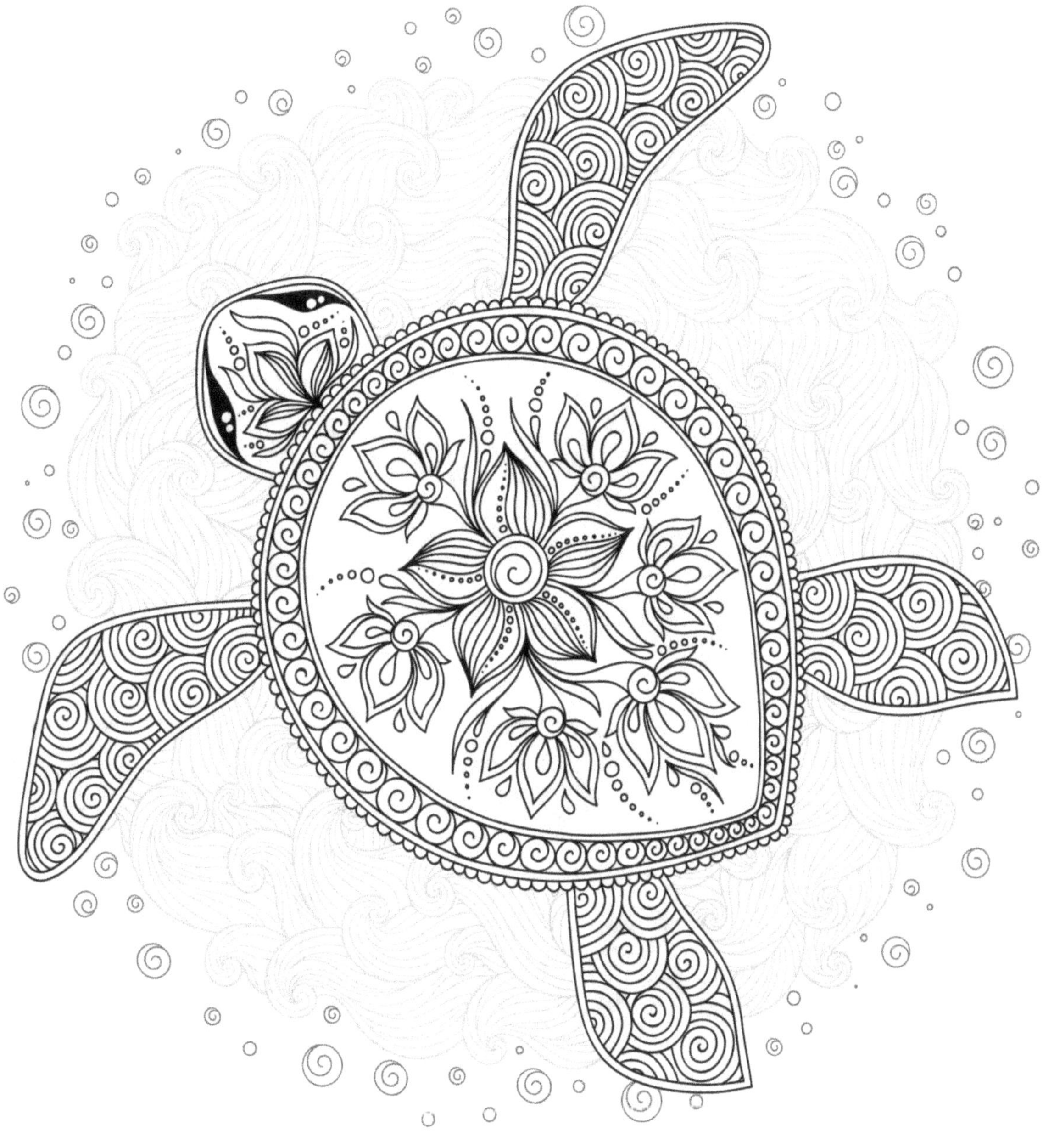

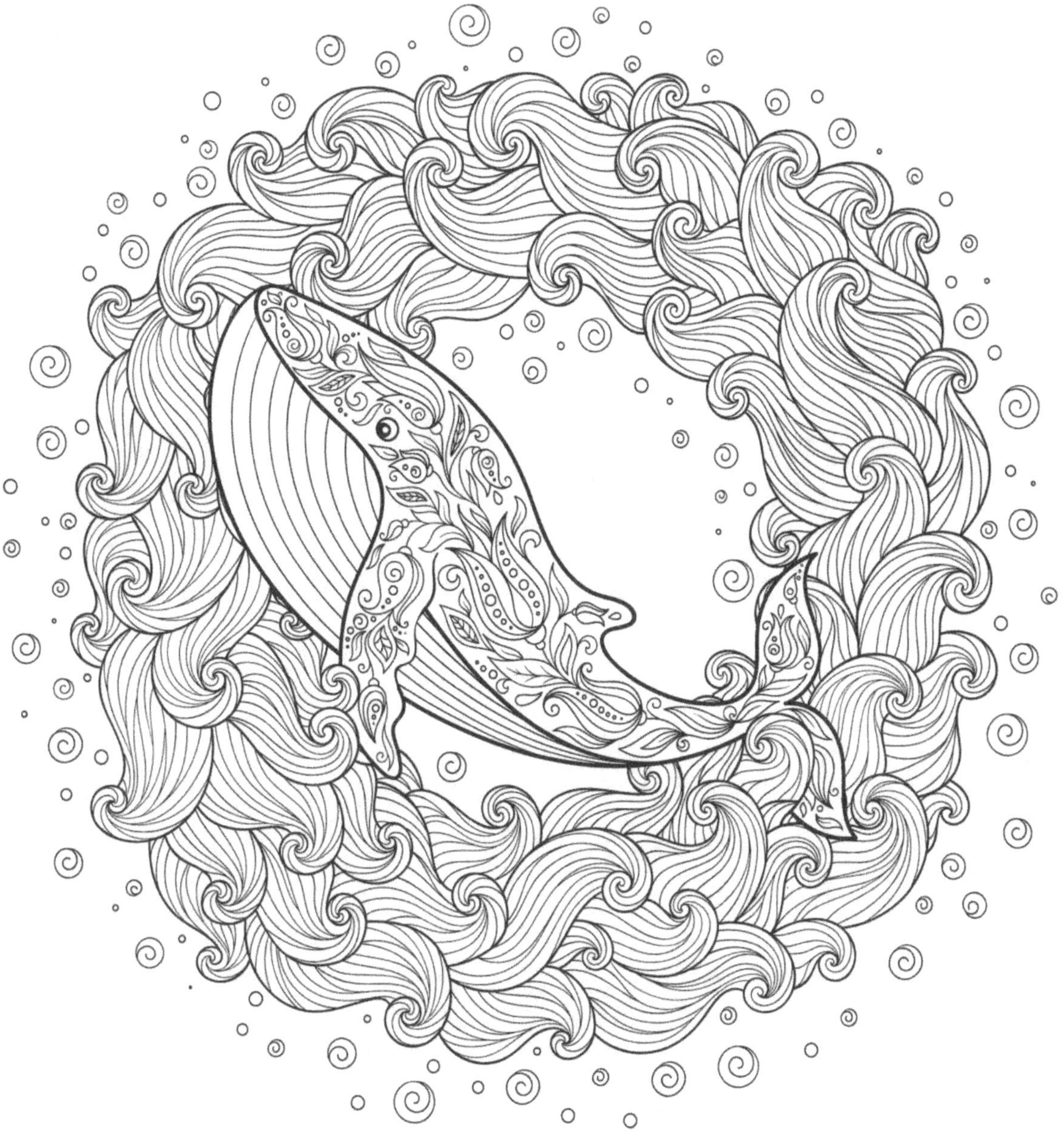

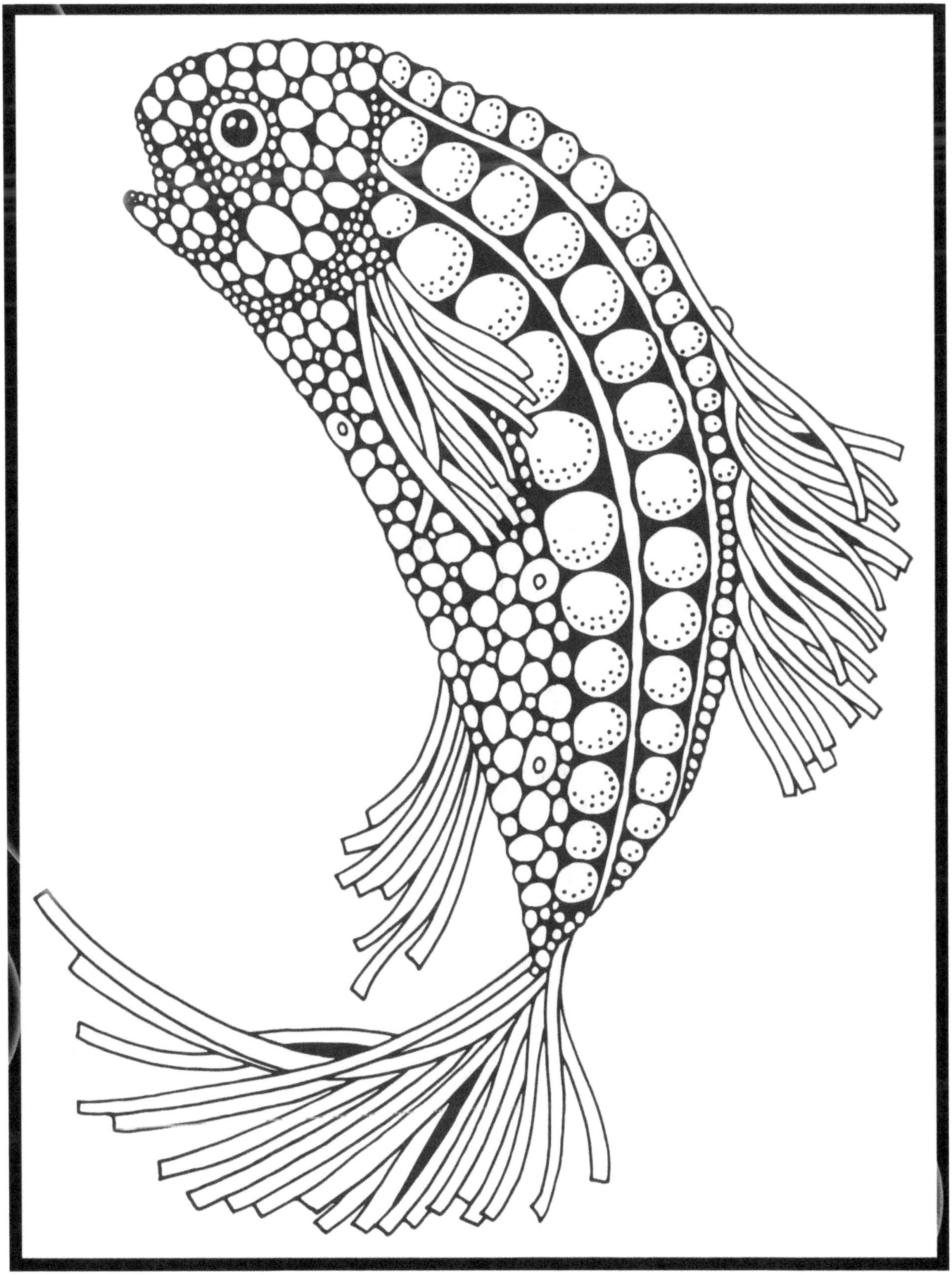

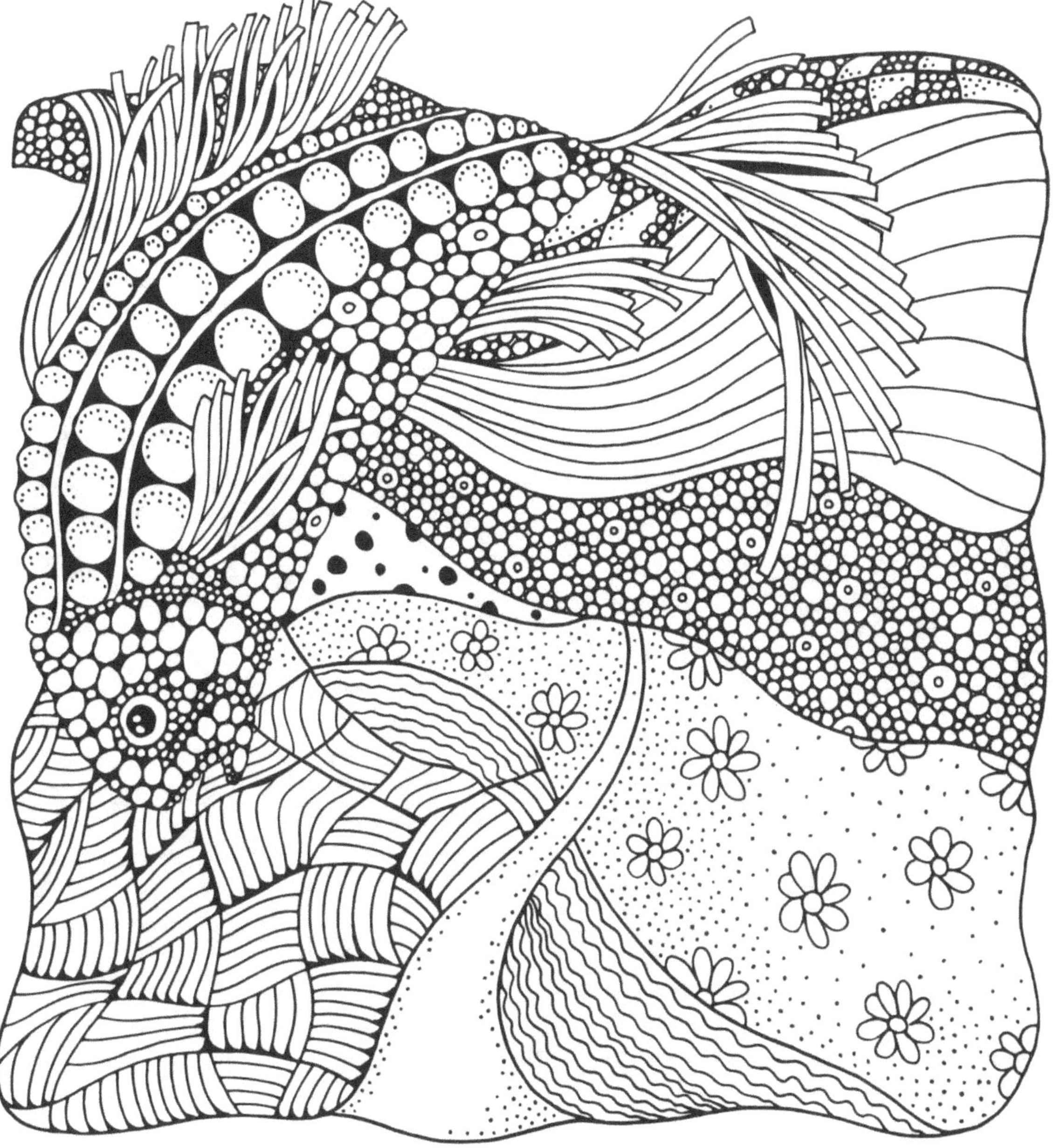

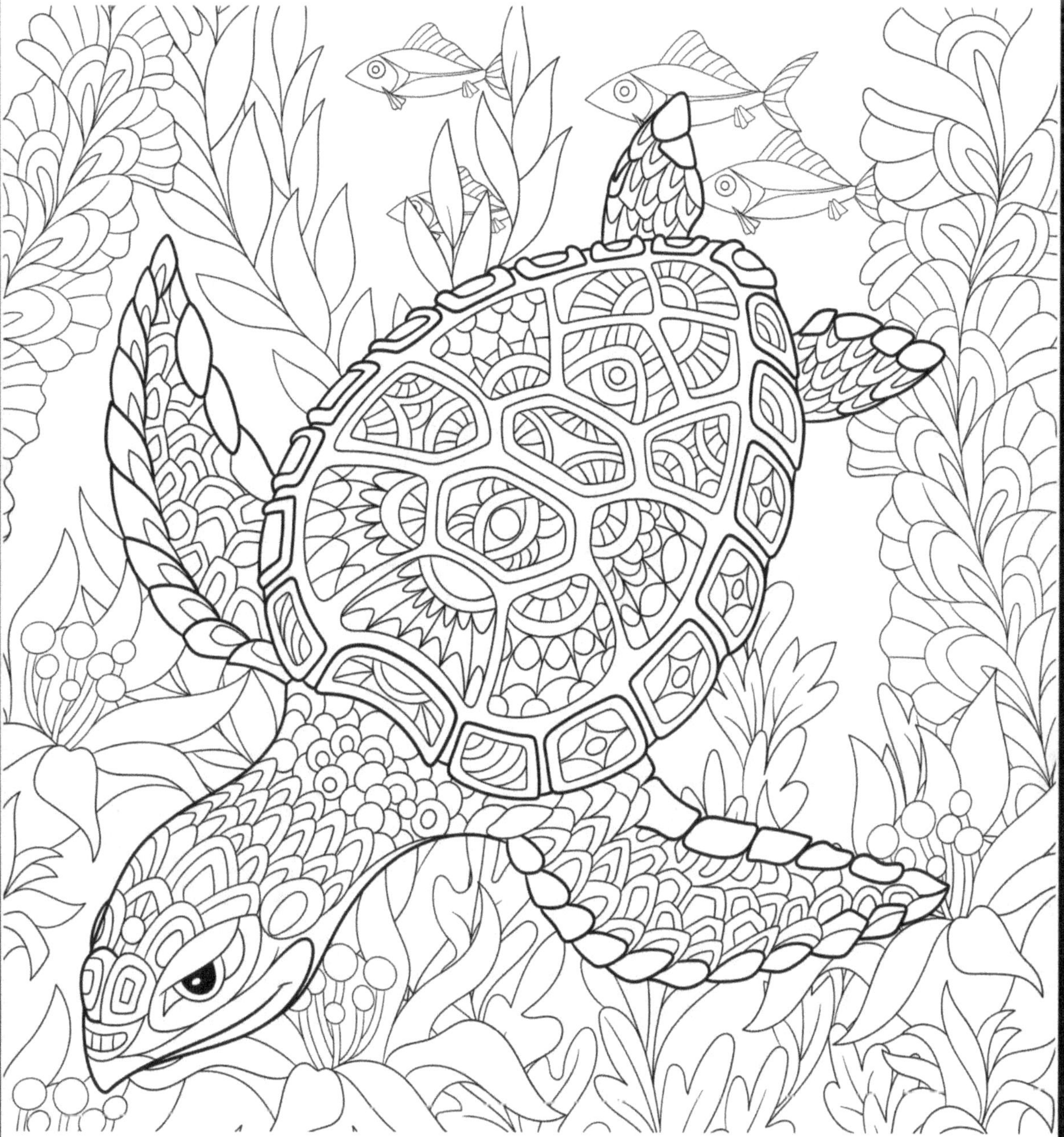

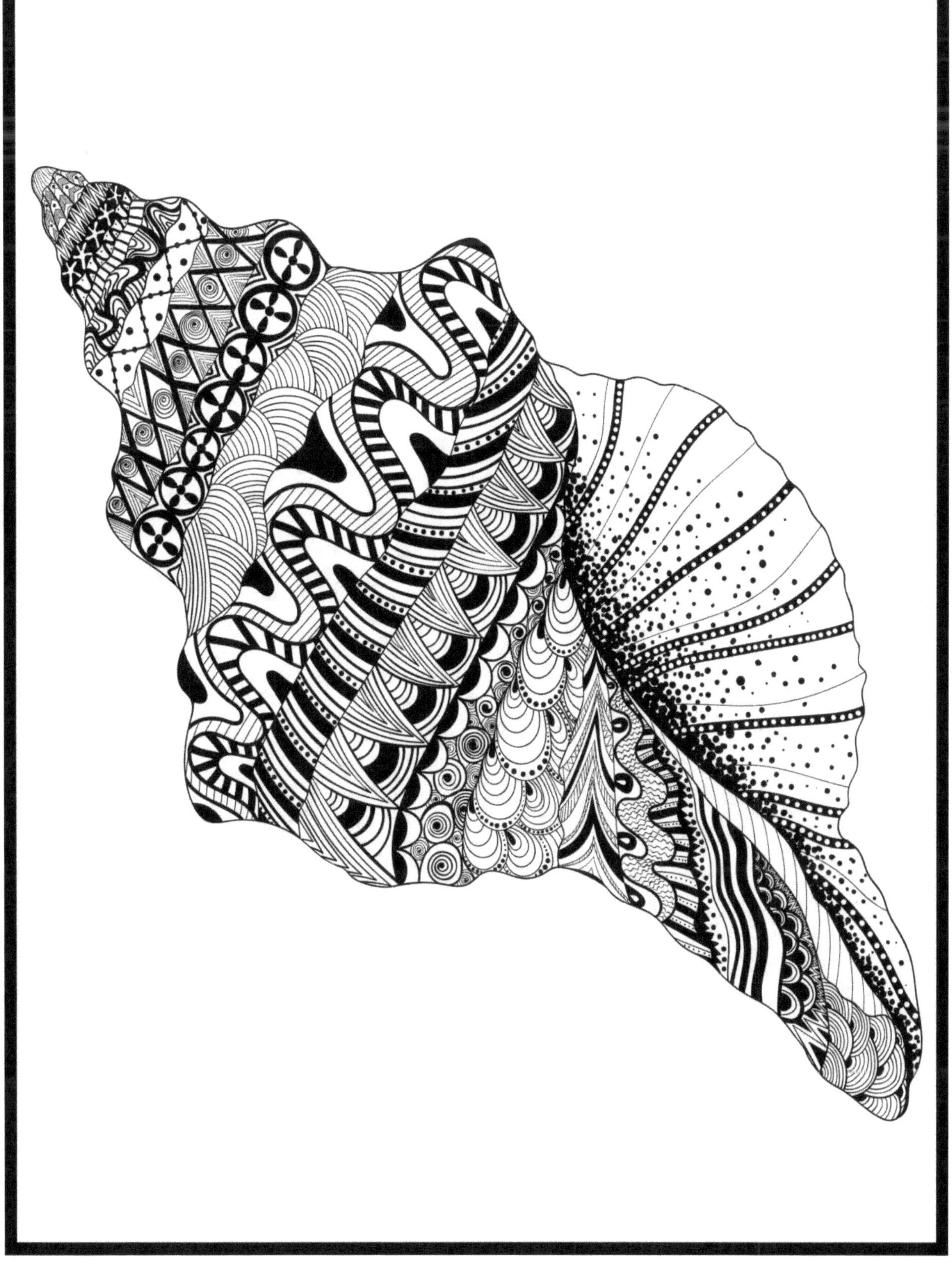

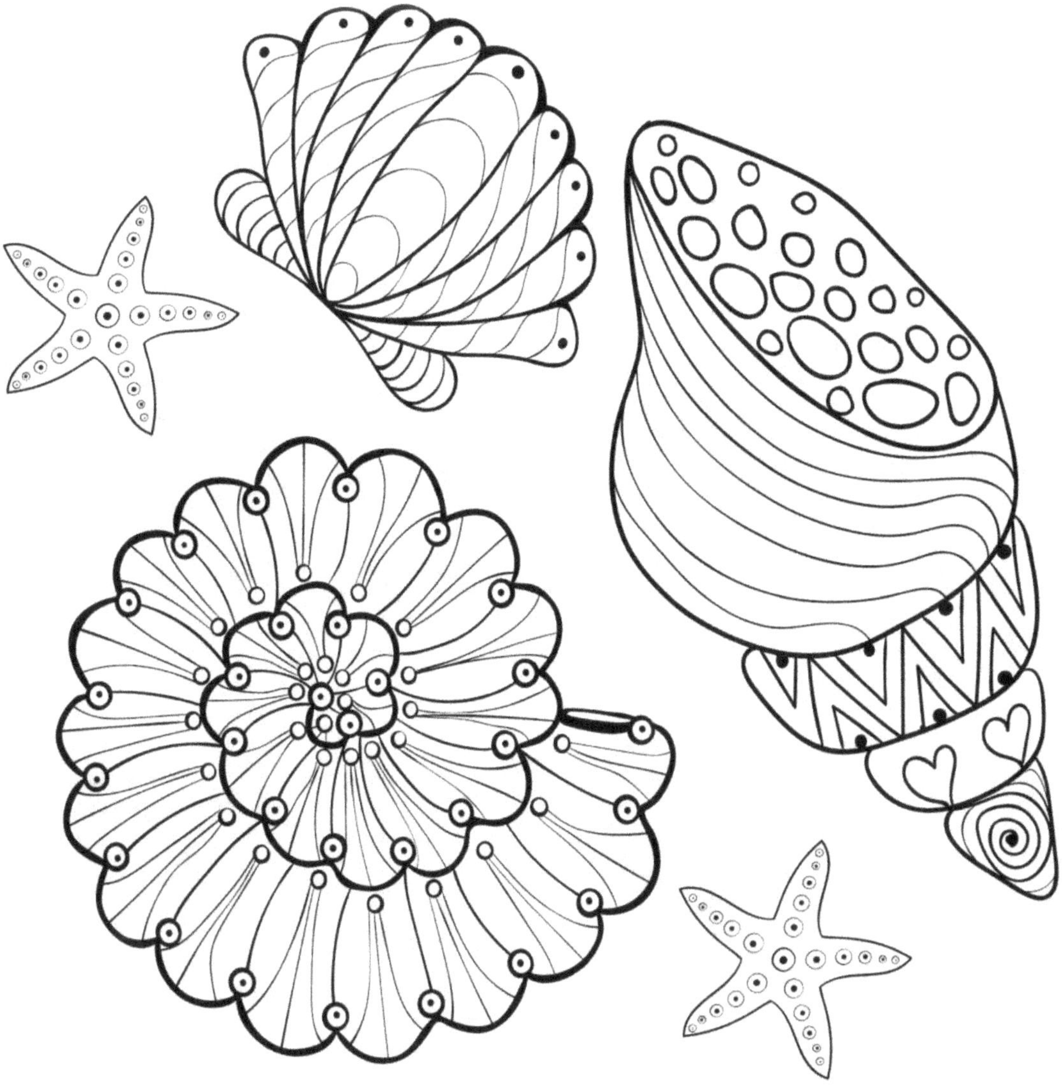

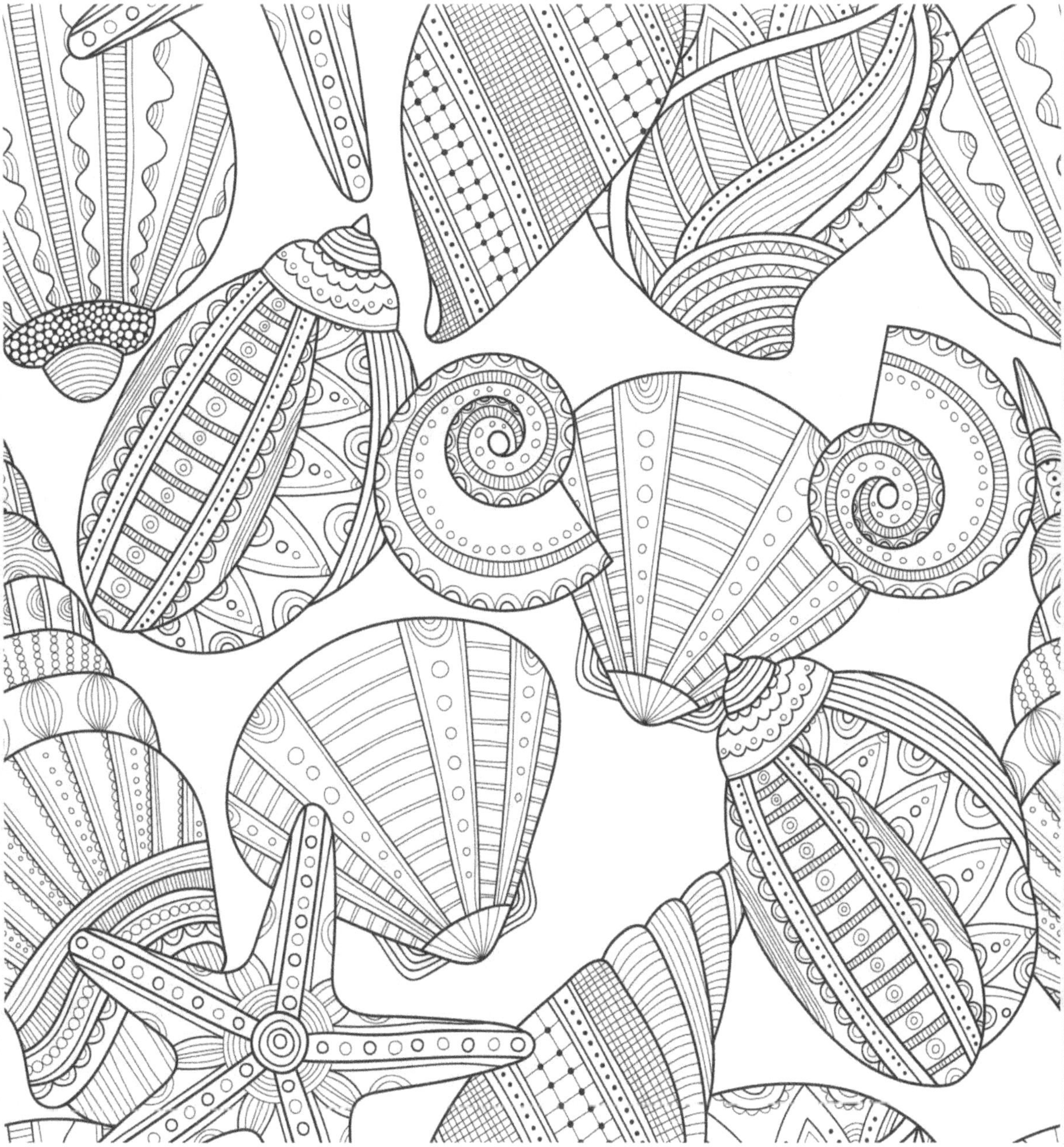

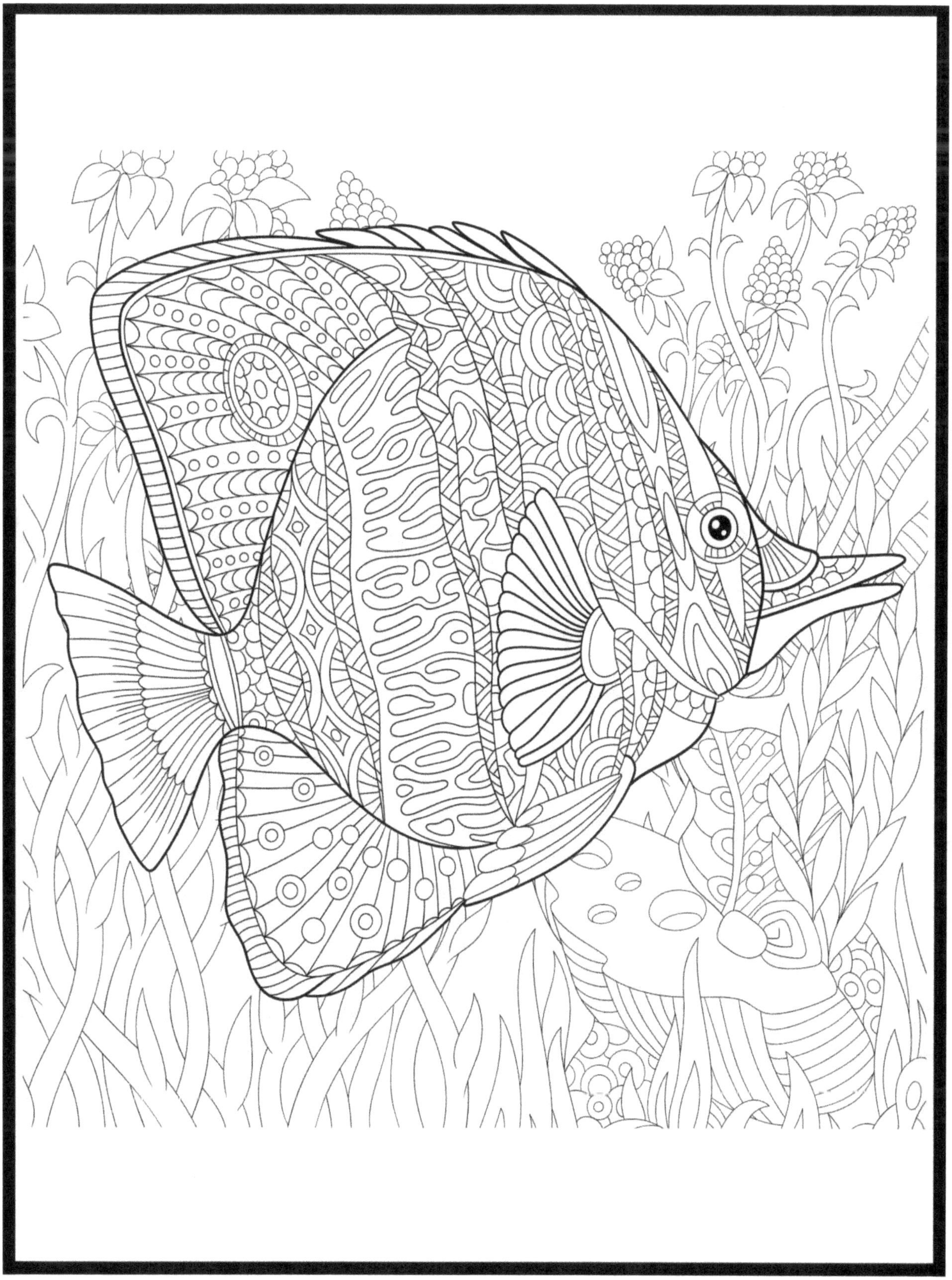

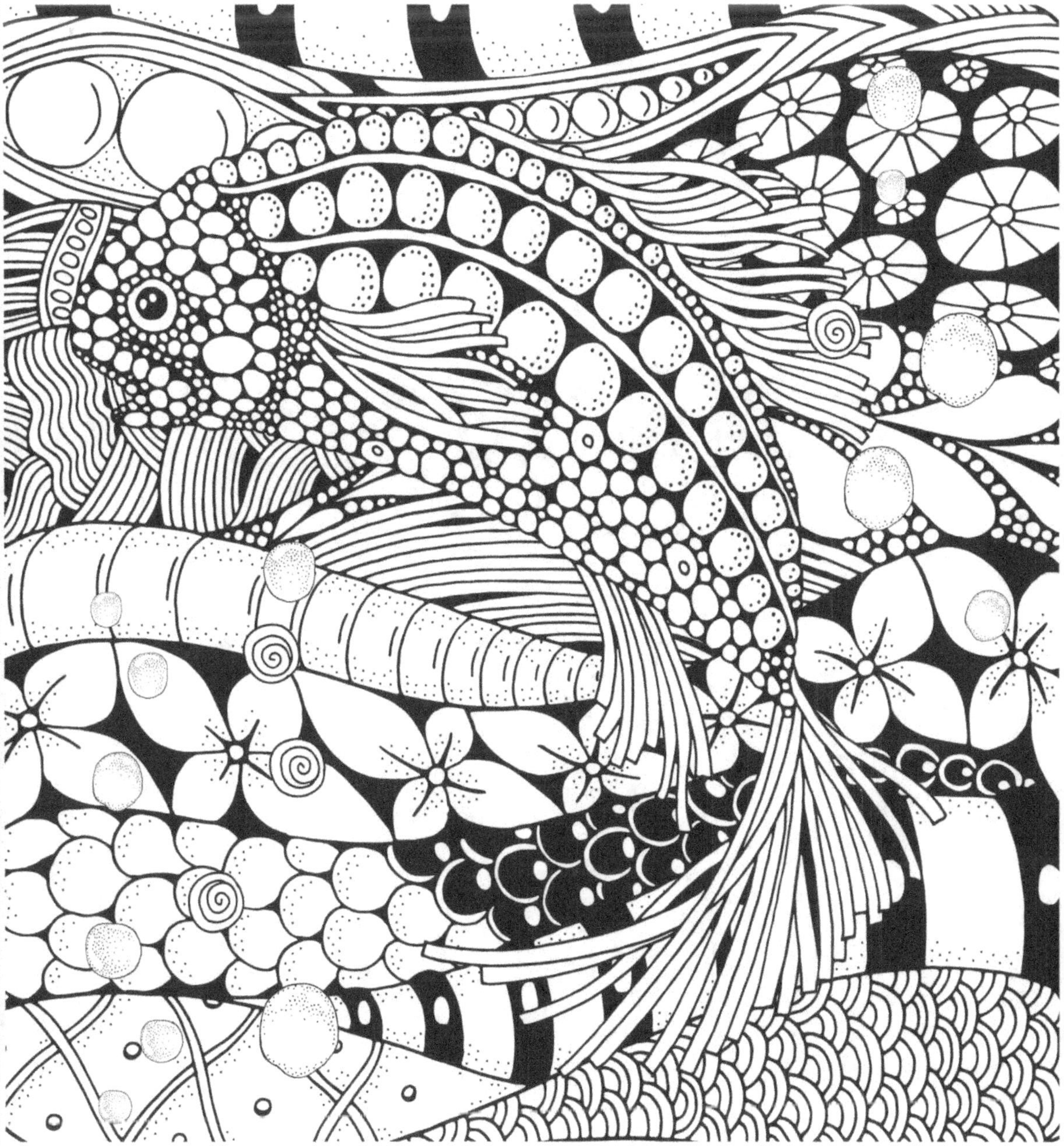

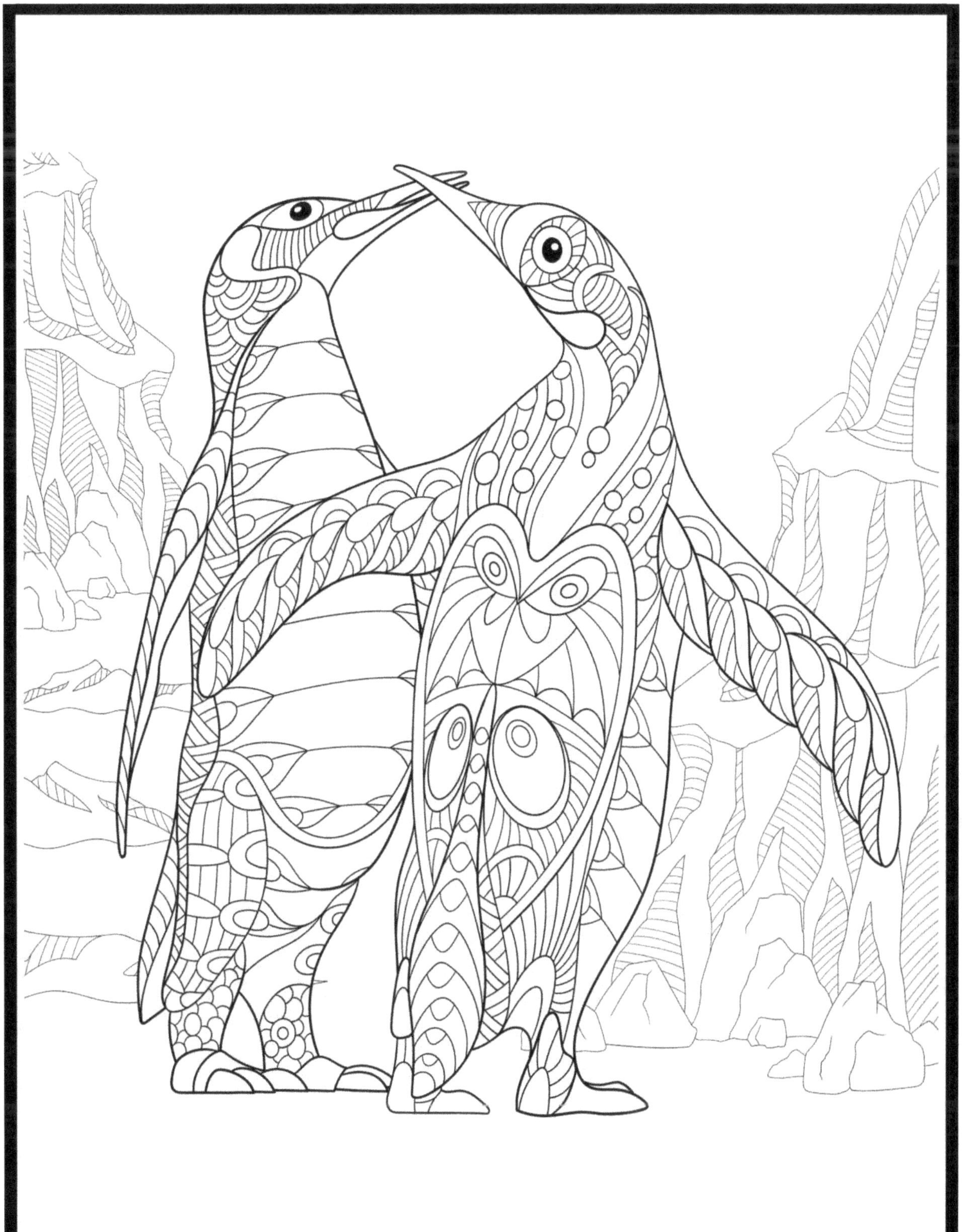

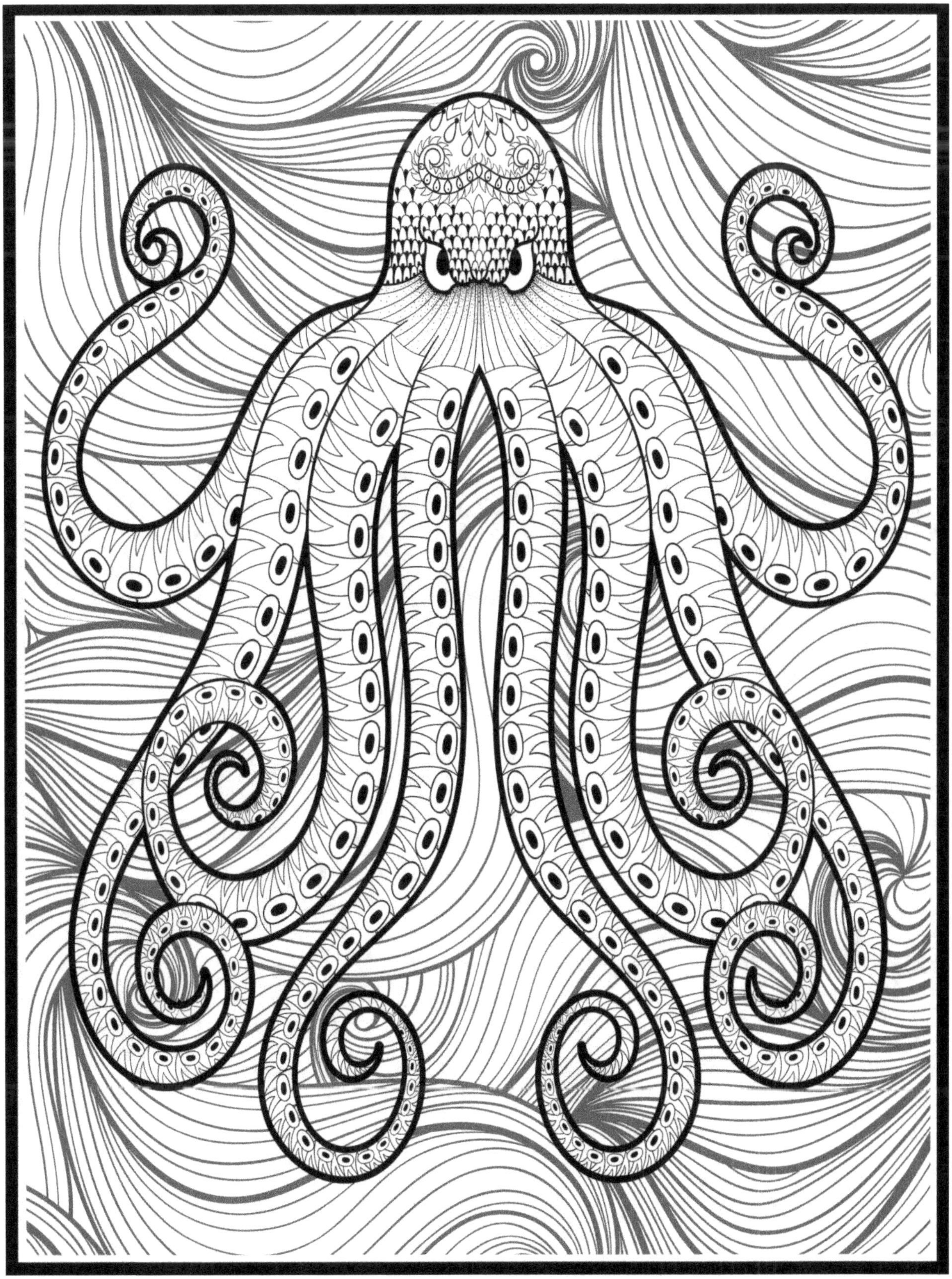

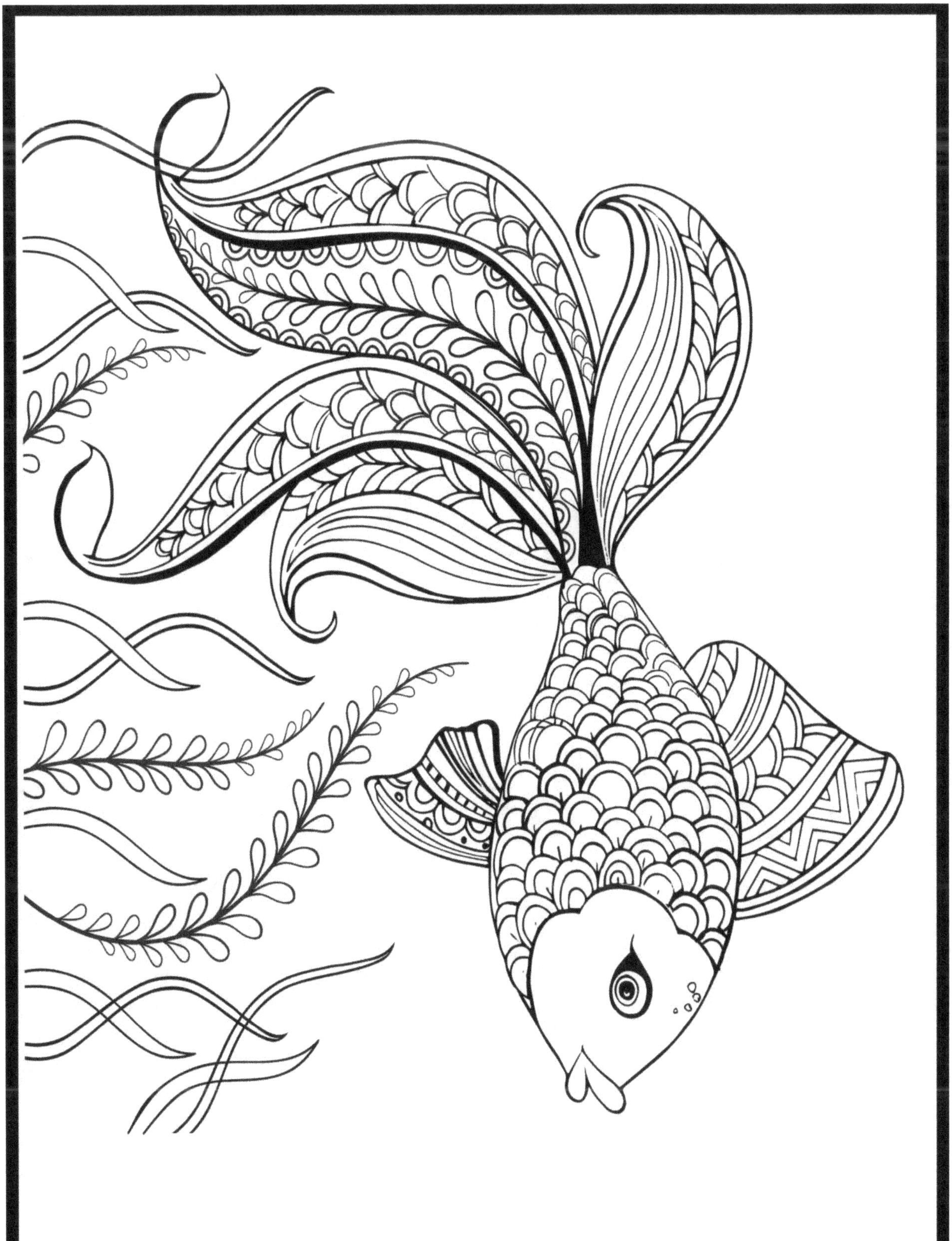

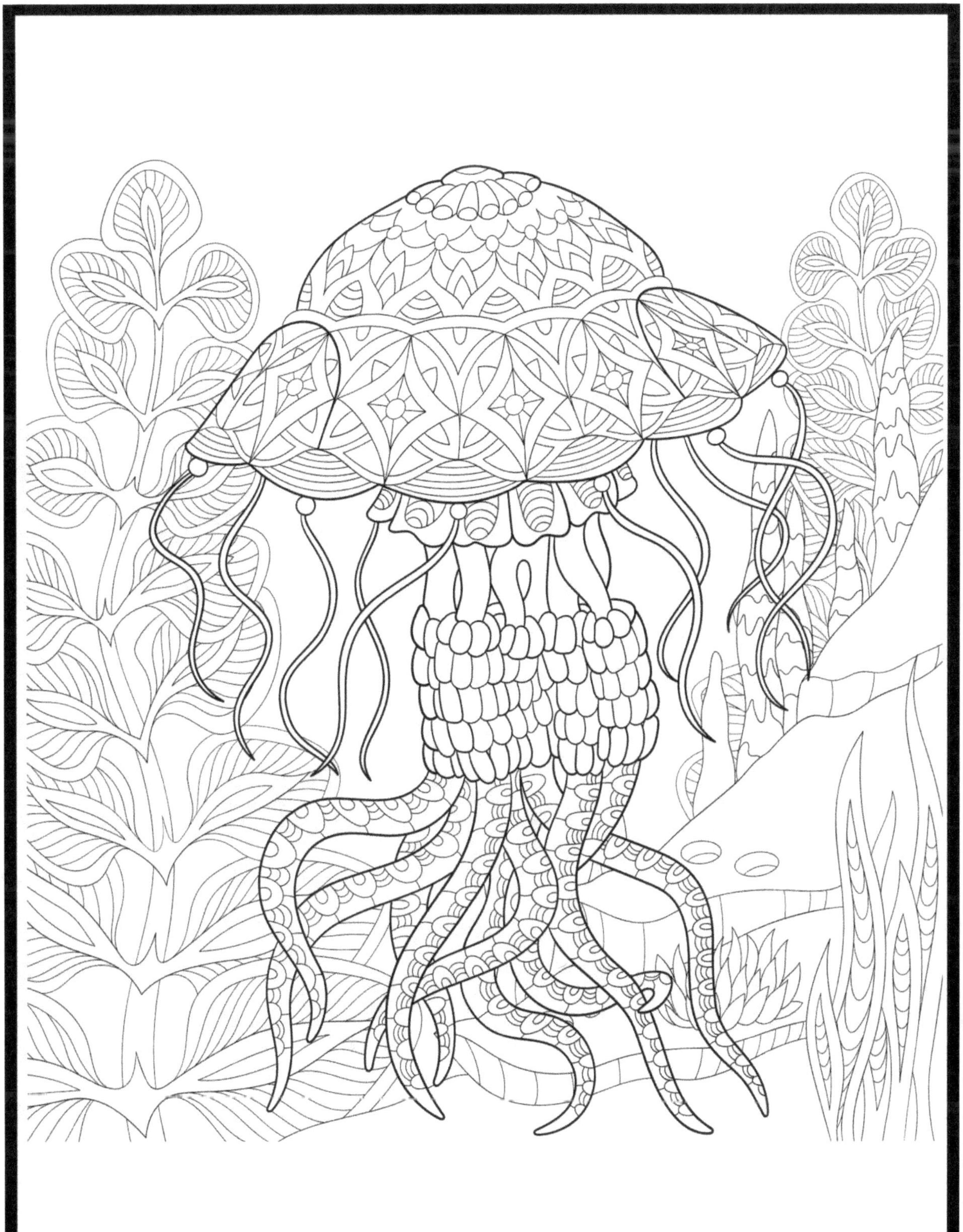

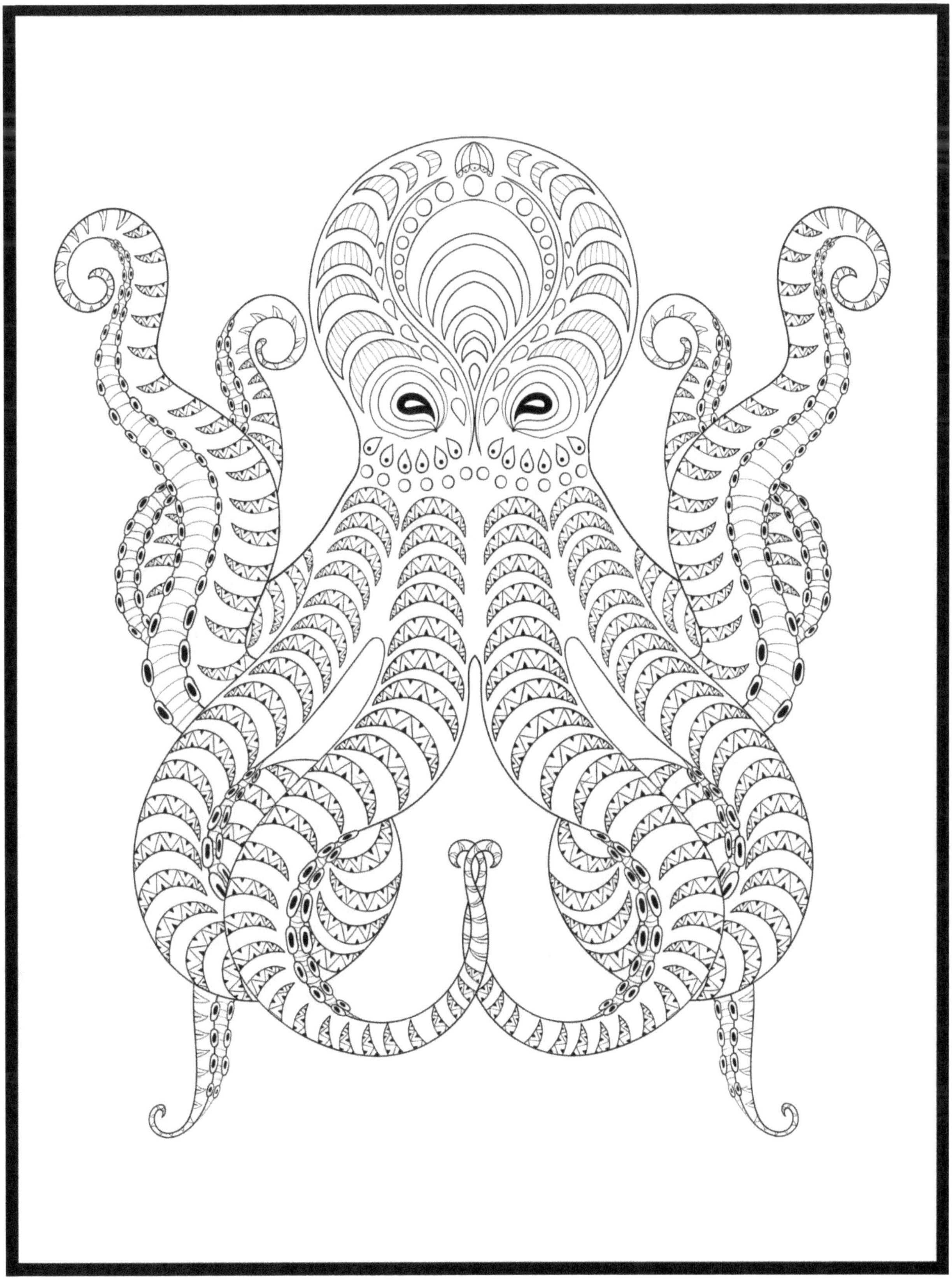

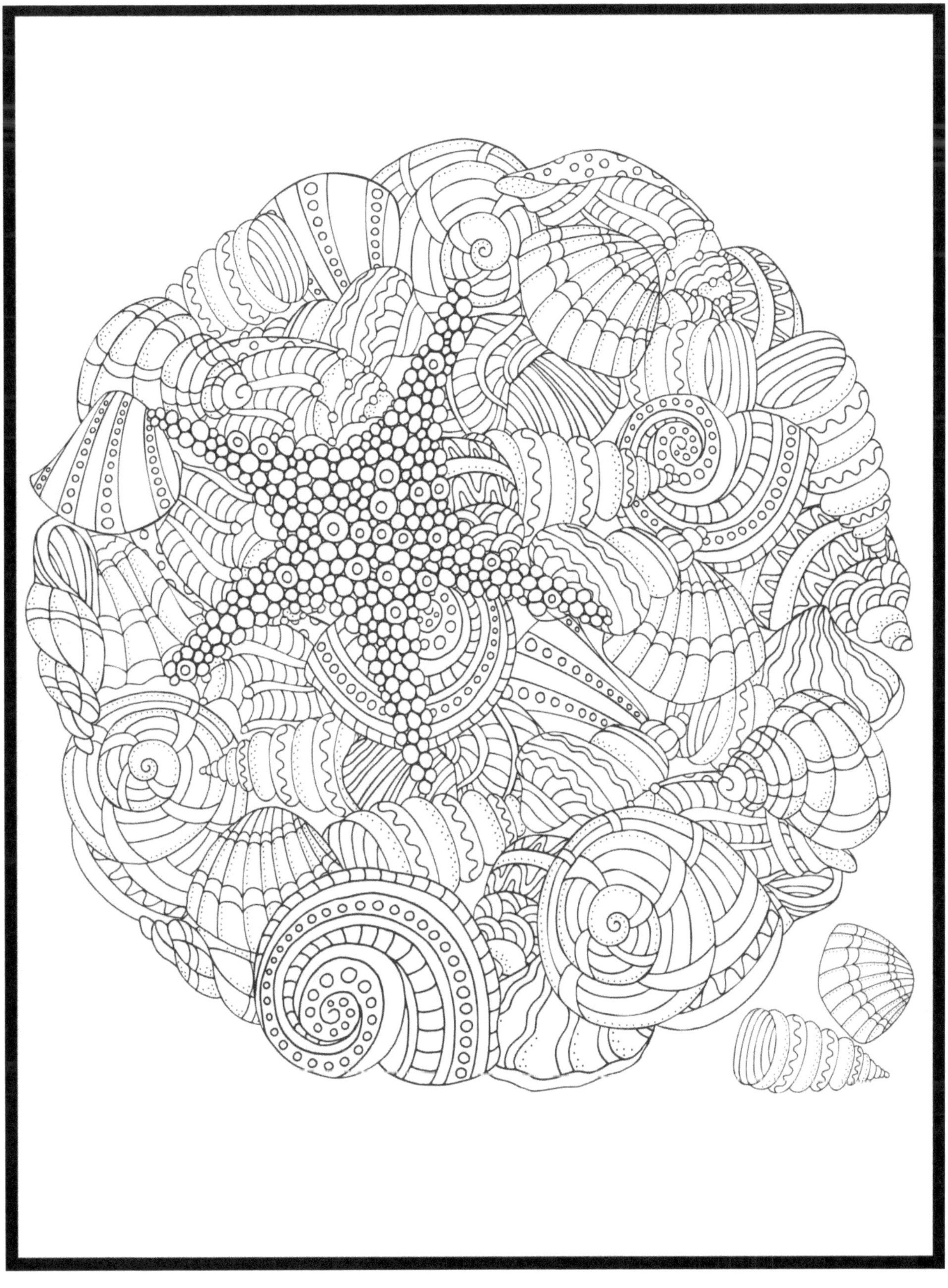

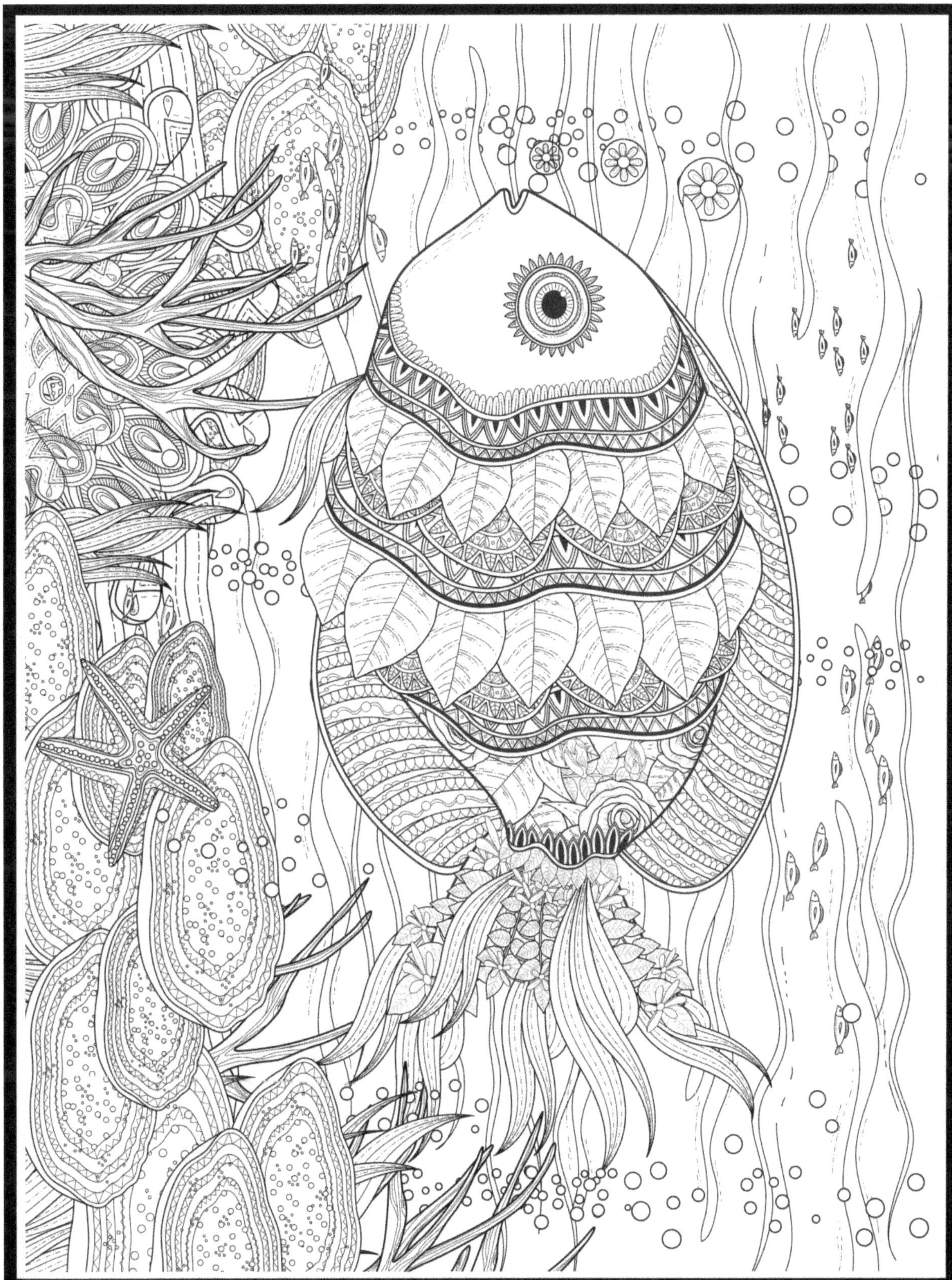

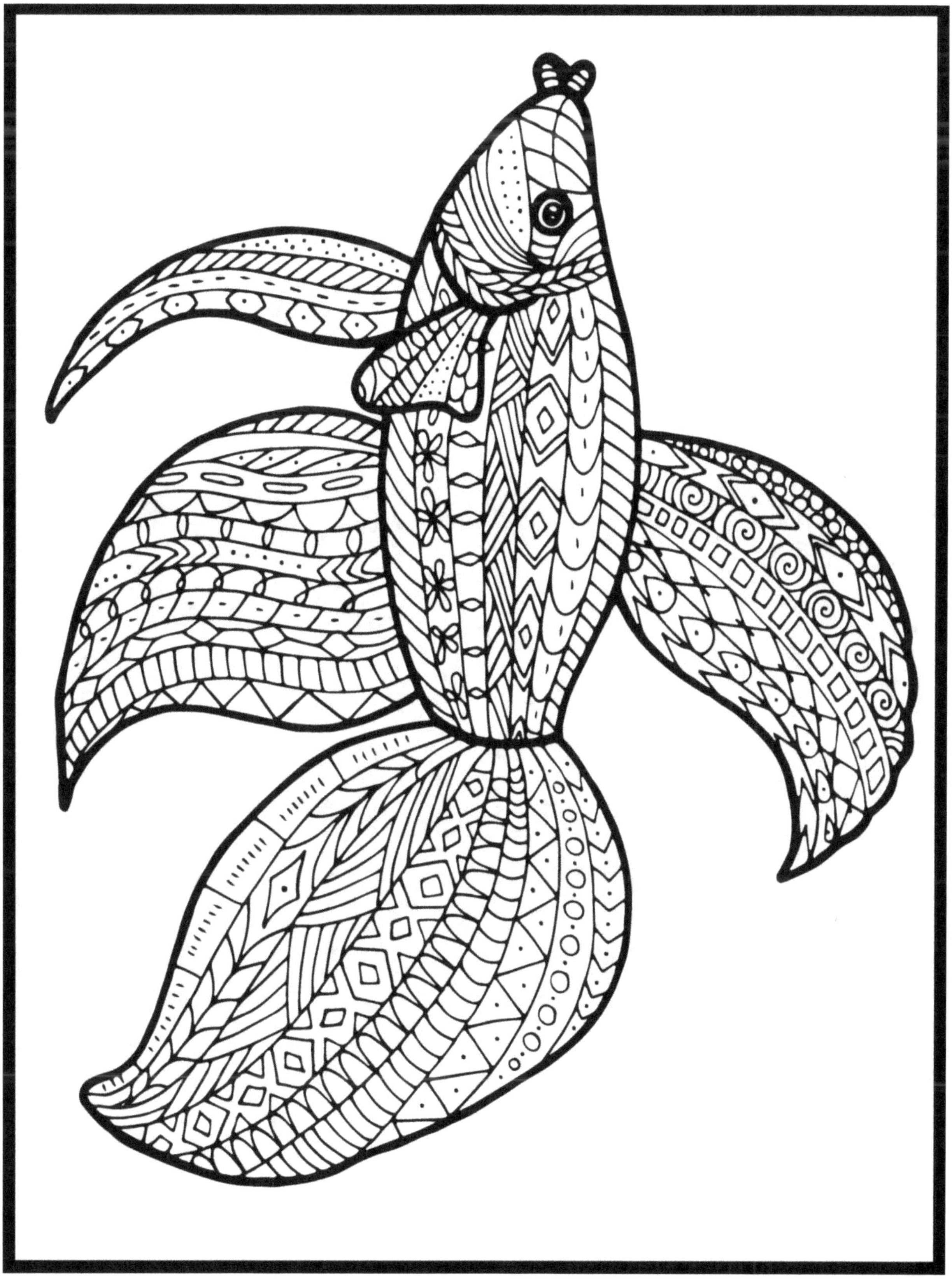

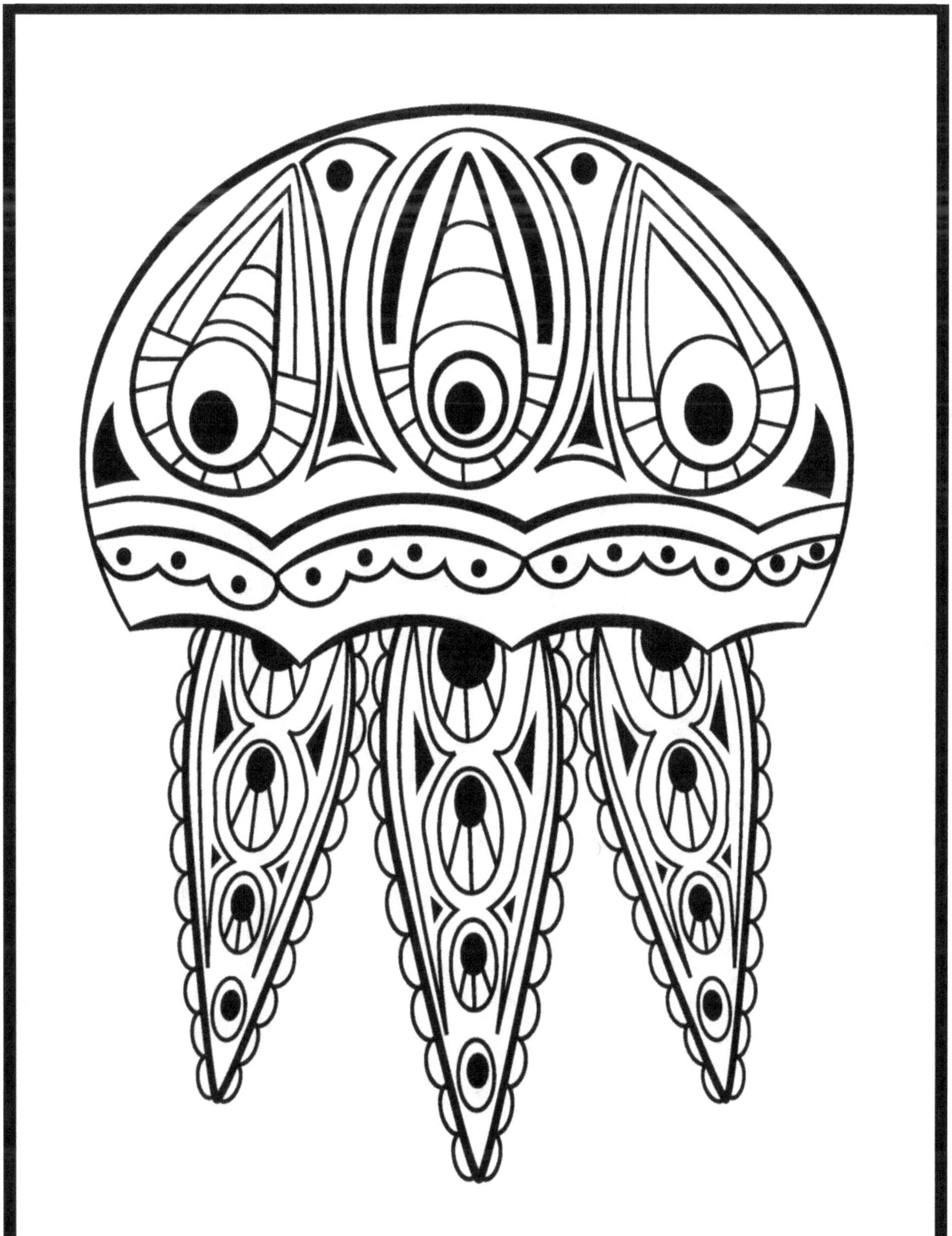

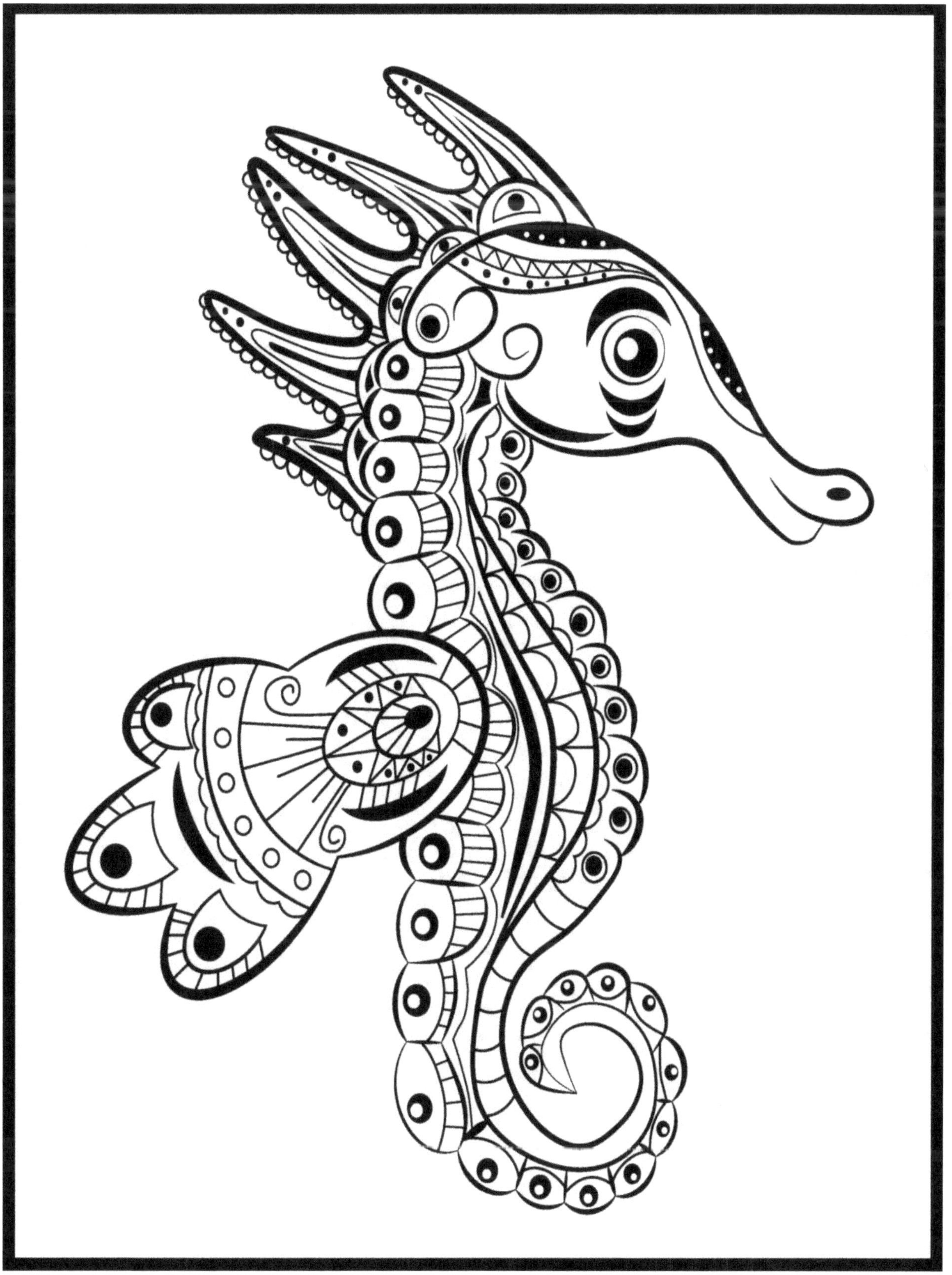

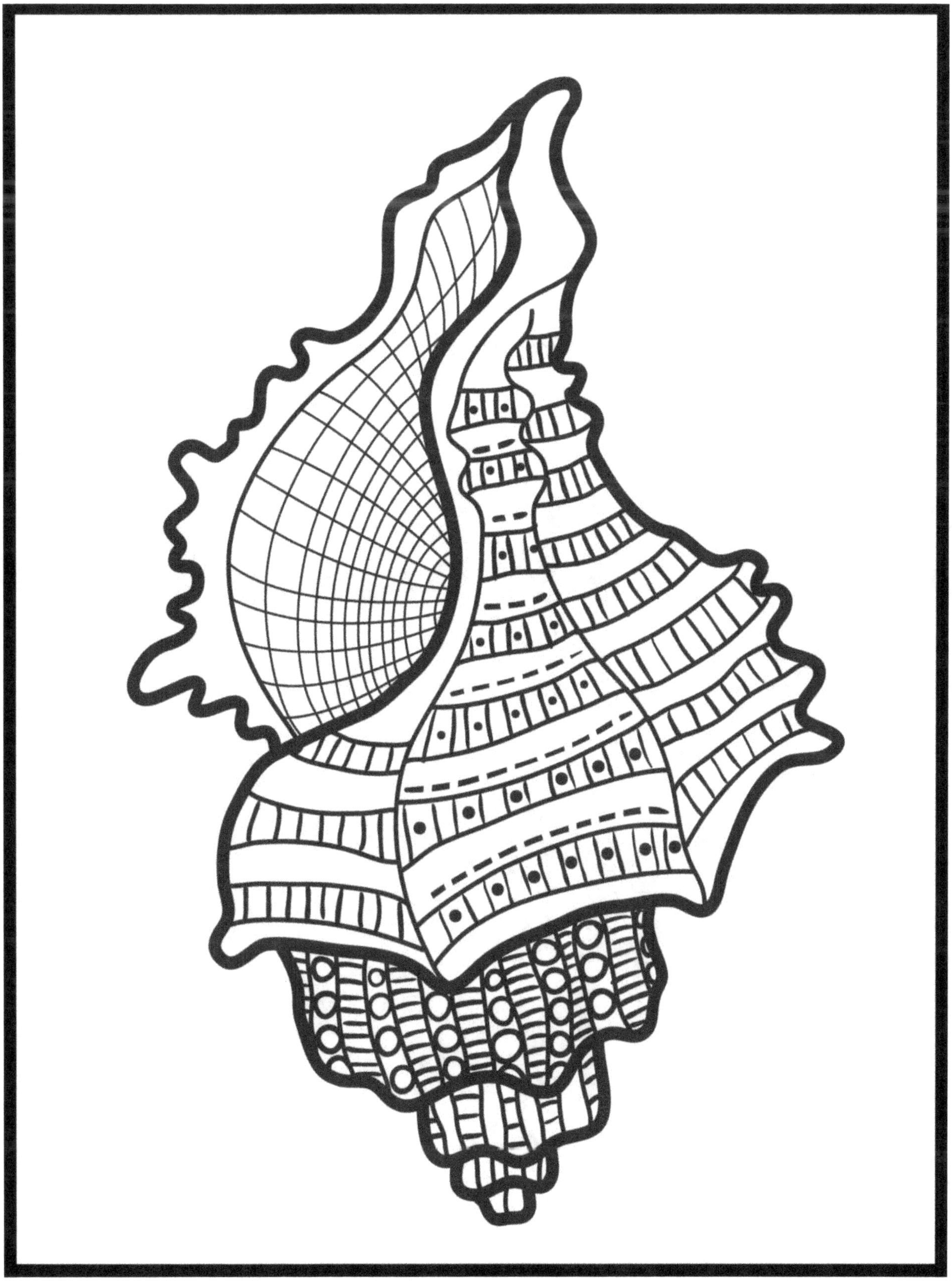

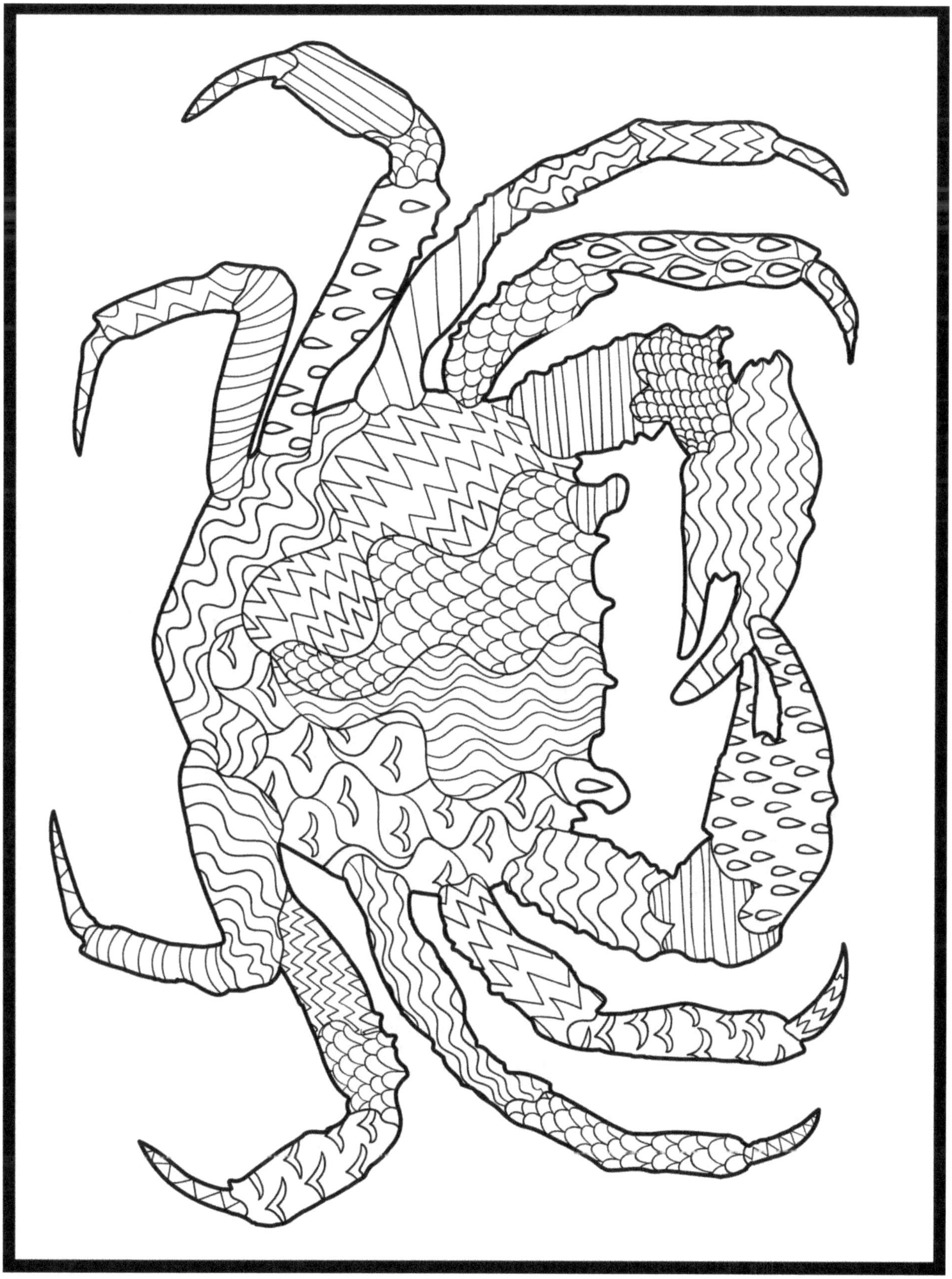

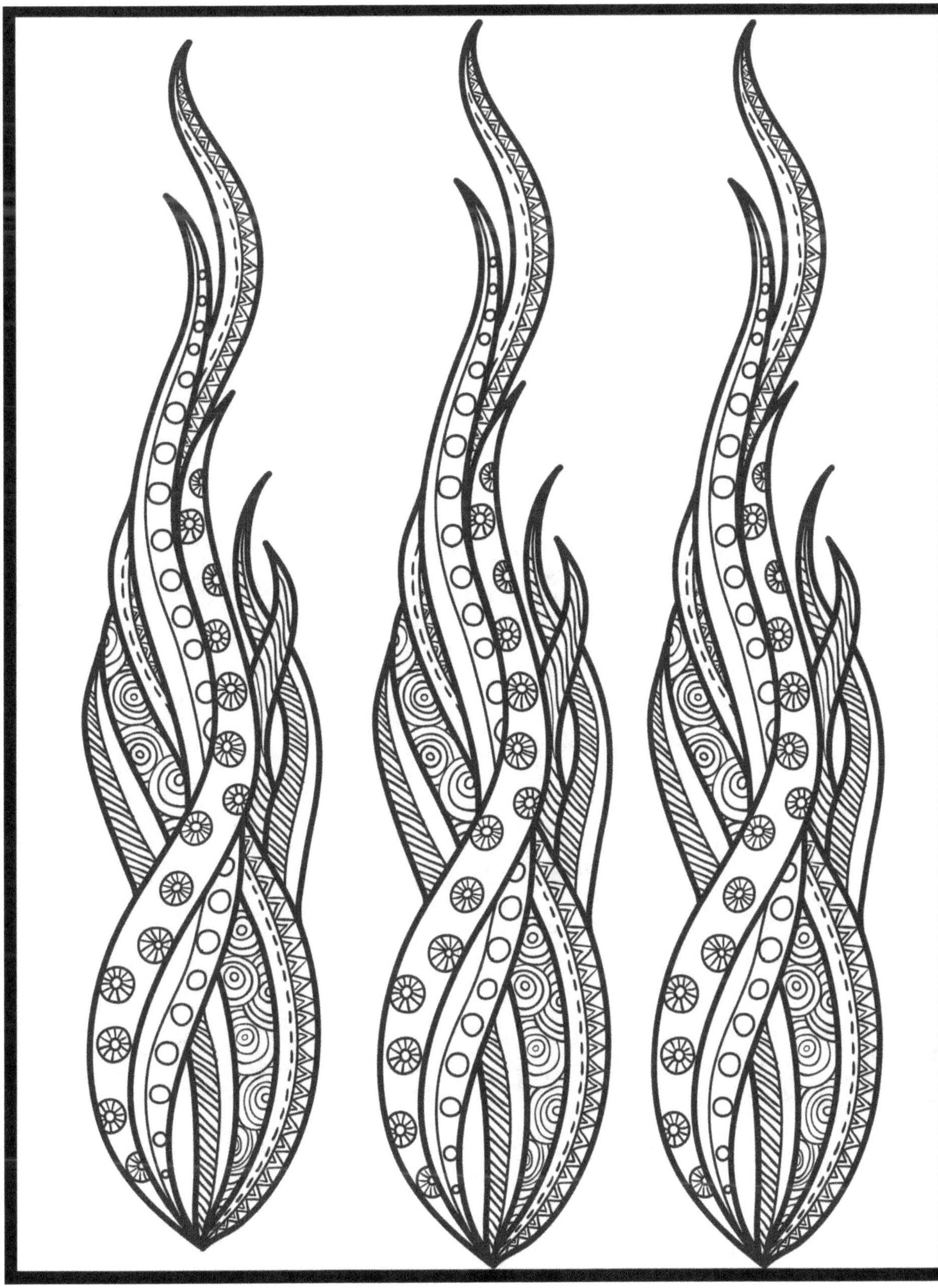

www.ingramcontent.com/pod-product-compliance
Lightning Source LLC
Chambersburg PA
CBHW081610220526
45468CB00010B/2834
* 9 7 8 1 7 2 0 7 2 5 3 1 2 *